21 Sept 2011

To   Hugh,

with compliments

from

Prem

Mutawaroo

PANGS OF LIFE

PANGS OF LIFE

Prem Kutowaroo

The Book Guild Ltd
Sussex, England

First published in Great Britain in 2003 by
The Book Guild Ltd
25 High Street
Lewes, East Sussex
BN7 2LU

Typesetting in Baskerville by
SetSystems Ltd, Saffron Walden, Essex

Printed in Great Britain by
Bookcraft (Bath) Ltd, Avon

A catalogue record for this book is
available from the British Library

ISBN 1 85776 796 9

CONTENTS

INTRODUCTION

'I am pleased to inform you that you've got the job, Mr Rey. Or shall I call you Prem?'

'Please call me Prem.'

'Do you want to ask me anything, Prem?'

'No sir.'

'Join the club then. You are part of the gang now, but don't call me sir. Call me Tony.'

'Sorry, sir – I mean Tony. It's a habit.'

'I know.'

I was very chuffed as I managed to thank Mr Tate, the interviewer.

'We'll send you information about the job by post and you can start next month. Can you do that?'

'Yes, Tony.'

'Well! We'll meet again. 'Bye.'

' 'Bye, Tony.'

It was a scorching Tuesday afternoon in January when I went for the interview in the city of Port-Louis in Mauritius. I had to wear a suit and tie, which was regarded as belonging to the middle or high class in the sixties. Then people used to wear suits only to work in offices. Otherwise, they were rare – and expensive. I was feeling ill at ease, wondering if I was wearing the tie right, and glancing around to see if people were looking at me. If someone was looking, I wondered if

1

something was wrong, especially as I had worn a suit only a few times before for interviews and because I was not an office worker. But I recalled Mr Tate saying, 'You look smart.'

Afterwards I sat in the botanical garden thinking about the interview. Mr Tate was a short, stockily built, stern-looking manager. The room where I was interviewed was small, with white-washed bare walls and only a table and five chairs. The setting had made me more nervous than I had previously realised. Besides, the way the manager had introduced himself was sufficient to imply that I had not got the job. But when he said I had got it, I was filled with emotion rather than thrilled.

For the interview, I had to travel by bus for 15 miles from a remote village (now non-existent) in the north of the island called Madame Louis (also known as Camp Masson). The bus took 45 minutes to reach the city along a winding and partly broken road. I was already sweltering when I arrived in Port-Louis and, because it is surrounded by a mountain range, there seemed to be no fresh air. It was boiling hot, with the temperature around 35 degrees centigrade.

I'd been to various interviews but didn't have much luck. Then I saw the advertisement for the road-mending job in a newspaper my uncle had brought from the town. I applied for it without any hope of getting it.

'You don't have to look for a job,' I remembered my uncle saying to me. 'I'm sure you're happy working for yourself. Besides, I need someone to help me on the farm!'

'No, uncle. I need to get a job because I don't want to be a burden to you.'

'You're not a burden, son. This is your place,' uncle said, trying to reassure me.

2

'But I want a job to go out and get to know life outside, uncle.'

'All right! All right! If that's what you want.'

My name is Prem Rey and I'd been unemployed for a few years after I left secondary school at 16. It was because, when I was a seven-year-old, my father died of a heart attack. My mother was left with me and my six-year-old sister called Devi – short for Devina. We were not rich and mother had to work harder than before in order to make ends meet. Sometimes I used to go and help her after school. I used to fetch water in pails or small drums from a canal that ran only a few hundred yards from the house. We used the water to cook our food and to give to the animals to drink. Mum used to wash our clothes at a river which ran parallel to the canal. Other times I used to help mum cut grass with a sickle from roadsides and fields to use as fodder for the cows and goats. If we cut grass far from the house, we used to tie it in bales and carry it home on our heads.

I used to walk on my own for nearly two miles to primary school in a pair of short trousers and a shirt (there was no uniform then) with my satchel on my back, containing a slate to write on with a pen made of slate. I used to cut through sugar cane fields and past the few houses in the school village, called Belle-Vue-Maurel. Sometimes passers-by used to stop to talk to me and wished me good day. I could remember always asking the time of a man on his bike in broken French (one of the languages spoken in Mauritius). He used to tell me the time but one day he stopped me and told me to ask for the time in proper French. I stopped asking for the time after that because I found out that he was a security guard at a water reservoir. As he was huge, he scared me and I thought that he would catch and lock me away if I persisted. It was considered

3

dangerous for a seven-year old to walk alone to and from school. But, I supposed, as I didn't have anyone to accompany me, it was thought acceptable.

In Mauritius, it was the custom, especially among people of Asian origin living in villages, to rear a couple of cows in a stable in order to get milk. I could recollect that we had three cows and five goats in the stable, about fifteen hens and two roosters roaming in the yard, and four pigs in the sty. All these animals and our house existed in four acres of land. The livestock provided us with milk, eggs and meat. We had sugar cane planted in three acres and this used to help make ends meet.

Looking after so many animals became a burden to my mother although she employed someone to help her out. Besides the hard work, mother also mourned the death of my father. She passed away a year after him. I was told that she died of heart failure, but I believe that she died more of exhaustion than heart failure. My sister and I didn't know what to do and who to turn to for assistance, but my uncle – my father's brother – volunteered to act as trustee.

'Is Uncle Ram looking after us?' Devina asked me.

'Yes, Devi.'

'I don't like him. He's fat and ugly. But I think he can take us out to the seaside and to the races.'

'No Devi, he is our uncle. We should like him. Did you hear how he talked to us yesterday? I think he's nice,' I tried to reassure her.

The death of my father was bad enough. We thought our mother was there to comfort us and help us wherever and whenever required, so her death came as a hard blow. Although my uncle volunteered to treat us like his own children, it was not the same. We knew

4

that we couldn't approach him like we did our parents. Yet we consoled ourselves by acquiring his trusteeship.

My uncle Ram wasn't privileged to have a farm like us. My parents had worked hard and managed to buy land. He had a wife and two daughters, was employed by a farmer in the next village and lived in a rented house. He chose to leave his job and move into our farm and look after it, and also my sister and me. He worked hard for some time and we both admired him for his work and dedication, although we cried for days on end for our parents. My uncle used to reassure us, telling us to treat him and his wife as our own parents.

There were two problems which I failed to notice, or noticed but couldn't do anything about. Firstly, my uncle wasn't a hard-working person like my father and, most of the time, the animals were left unattended or undernourished until most of the hens died and we were left with only one cow.

'I wish uncle looked after our animals better than he is doing,' said Devi. She was quite chatty and observant for her age.

'I know,' I replied. 'He should look after them properly.' On the other hand, my auntie was constantly nagging my uncle for some unforeseen – at least to us – reasons. In addition to this, he hardly ever took us on holidays, to the seaside or even to relatives, as our parents occasionally had. These were probably the reasons why we couldn't take to our uncle like our parents.

I admired my uncle for looking after us but I couldn't tell him about the problem of leaving the animals unattended because it was a principle that elders were respected and couldn't be approached. We were getting on well with my auntie but there were some problems with her daughters, especially regarding my sister. Devi used to tell me how those girls bullied her and threatened to beat her up for no reason. I felt obliged to protect Devi but, being a child myself, I felt weak and daunted. We used to hug each other and cry ourselves to sleep.

At one stage, Devi said that our auntie didn't like her. We didn't take much notice of this because, although we thought she was siding with the girls, uncle and auntie were our elders and couldn't be approached, even if uncle had told us to do so whenever we needed something. Sometimes we would think, What's the point! They're living on our property. We would console ourselves that the elders were more experienced than us, the children.

We prayed every day for something positive to happen. We couldn't understand where we went wrong, or why God had forsaken us, in order to deserve such a life. The loss of our parents was bad enough, but acquiring a trustee who we couldn't approach was unimaginable. There was no one else we could turn to. We were kids and everyone was older than us. No one came to visit us as often as they used to in the days of our parents. We were living in a different world. The existing world was precarious. There was a mixture of heaven and hell. We believed that hell was predominant.

'God, there must be an end to all this,' I mused in disgust sometimes. I used to remember that my dad used to say, 'Prem, there is always a light at the end of the tunnel.' I didn't know its meaning at that time, but if there was a light, I couldn't see it. It was non-existent. I despaired, but I still thought the light might appear in the future.

One afternoon my uncle appeared.

'Prem, Devi. I've come to talk to you. Are you all right?'

6

We both nodded without saying anything.

'I've been noticing that something has been bothering you. I've told you to approach me as you would your dad. Don't worry about anything. Talk to me as you would have with your father. Besides, I am his brother. Shiv was a nice person and so was your mum.'

'Yes, uncle,' we replied.

'I've some plans which I've talked over with your auntie. I'm sure they will be in your best interests.'

I thought that, after all, there was a light, but, because he didn't tell us what plans he had in mind, it worried us to a great extent. I mulled over a lot of ideas. At first, I thought that he was going to work hard to recover what he had lost at the farm, but that was proved wrong because it was his nature to be slack and I knew that a leopard wouldn't change its spots. We also thought that he might talk to his daughters about their attitudes towards Devi but that was also not forthcoming either. We also thought of other possible plans until we gave up.

The morning after my uncle talked to us, we saw both uncle and auntie going out. They came back late in the evening. The following day a car pulled in and a couple in their late thirties – I was hopeless at judging someone's age – emerged. It so happened that Devi and I were feeding the pigs in their sty. They greeted us.

'Good afternoon. How are you, children?'

'We're fine, thank you.'

As soon as they had greeted us, our uncle and auntie came out and called them inside. After a lengthy talk with both uncle and auntie, they departed. We couldn't understand what was going on. At first, we thought that they might have been some acquaintances, but that was the first time we had seen those people around. In the

7

end, we settled into thinking that they were some visitors.

When they had gone, uncle came to see us again.

'How did you like the people who came to see you?'

They came to see us? I didn't even know they came to see us, I thought to myself.

'They looked all right.'

'Good,' he said, and left us.

Then, for some strange reason, an odd notion came to my mind. I started thinking. Why come to see us? Are we for sale? I know that people go to see an animal, such as a goat or a cow, before they buy it. They aren't buying us, are they?

I still couldn't ask uncle what was going on. I also thought, Is he trying to get rid of us so that he will get hold of the farm, after applying the softly-softly approach last night? For God's sake, can someone tell us and put our minds at rest.

I didn't understand. Besides, now I was eight years old, and these ideas were mysteries overlaid with heart-ache and uncertainties.

The following morning one of my uncle's daughters said that Devi wouldn't be there long. At first I thought that was another of their pranks and didn't take much notice of it.

These events made us feel that our world was shrink-ing and that both Devi and I were being squeezed into a cage. Whereas before we could express ourselves to our uncle in our own ways, now we preferred to keep ourselves to ourselves. Life was becoming grim and full of uncertainties. I had never heard of child suicide, but if matters were to get any worse, there was going to be a suicide pact. I didn't think that seven-year-old Devi could understand much about the world's weird occurrences but I had an idea of what was happening. I remembered my father's words about the light.

It seemed that our uncle couldn't see what a terrible state we were in yet he wanted to talk to us when he came to see us again the following evening.

'How are you, my children?'

'We're fine, thank you.'

'I'm sorry I had to leave you yesterday. I couldn't speak to you then. I've to tell you that I'm having Devi adopted.'

1

Separation Through Adoption

The dilemma to adopt Devi or to keep her had been a nagging problem to our uncle. But the news was a bombshell to us.

'Does this mean that she's going to stay at a relative's place,' I inquired.

'No, son. I don't think you understand. To adopt means taking up the responsibility of a child by a different family to their own.'

I couldn't ask him any other question because he was, I thought again, much older than me.

'Yes. I've to have her adopted for your and her best interests. You see me like this. Well! Probably you do not know it, but I'm a diabetic and I have to take medicine regularly for it. Some years ago I had a sore on the big toe of my left foot. Then it became infected and spread up the leg no matter how well I cared for my feet. The toes became gangrenous and, because the doctor feared that might spread further, he preferred to amputate the leg below the knee.'

I had a shock of my life when he showed us his left leg. He had a wooden leg fitting so that he could walk well. This accounts for his limp and sluggishness, I thought to myself. Now I realised why he was slow with his work. I had previously thought that he was less active than my father. This was the first time I felt sorry

11

for him. I couldn't tell how Devi felt, but I could see her staring at the leg as if her eyes would fall out the sockets. Probably, the idea of adoption had escaped her mind temporarily.

'Don't think we're using your farm for our own benefit. That's not the case. You see, your auntie nagged me into adopting Devi. She's not well herself because she has cancer. I don't expect you to know what cancer is. It's a disease that eats a person inside until that person dies. Remember we had a visitor? Well! They came to see Devi. They liked her. We didn't want to tell you anything in case you got worried.'

Worried? What does he know about getting worried? I thought to myself. I felt sorry for his misfortunes, but at the same time, I felt like slapping him for not telling me such awful news. I didn't think he should be telling us such horrible things, especially at our age. We didn't understand much at that time, but I later realised that he had to tell us to make us understand it better.

'Your auntie has only a year or two to live,' added my uncle. 'She doesn't know it. The doctor told me and, if I tell her, she'll worry a lot and probably die before her time.'

This was another blow. It was the first time I had seen uncle crying.

He then said in a choking voice, 'I thought I'd tell you now so that you won't blame me for anything later. I know you're still kids and you've just lost your parents yourself. I could've kept Devi here, but as she's a girl, I thought it would be best for her to start a new life. Who knows! She'll be better off in her new home. You'll miss each other for a while. After that, you'll be fine, I hope. Your auntie may not be here.'

I was wondering how he would account for her

spiteful daughters when, as if he read my mind, he added, 'When she goes, I'll be left with Koosh and Parm – my daughters. They are here as my support and they are young. They don't understand the pace of life. If something happens to them, I'll be responsible. It's all right for you, you're a boy. But if something happened to Devi, I'd never forgive myself. Think about it. One day, when you grow up, you'll know exactly what I'm trying to tell you.'

After such a lengthy and depressing speech, my uncle left. Devi and I stared at each other, speechless, with tears in our eyes.

Shall we run away? I thought. But where to, though? Perhaps uncle was right. Then I thought that I might have the opportunity to visit Devi and that she would visit me. We would keep in touch by letters (there was no telephone).

It was nearly eight o'clock in the evening and just coming to bedtime. Usually we used to be in bed by nine, but that night we weren't feeling tired. We stood looking at each other, speechless, as if we were struck by lightning. Then, as if drawn by magnets, we found ourselves in an embrace, with tears streaming down our cheeks. We were lost for words. We just stayed in an embrace for ages. After what seemed an hour, we dropped off to sleep, but that sleep was intermittent and nightmarish. We wanted to talk but we remained quiet. At about five – I knew the time because roosters started crowing around then – I was wide awake.

'Devi . . . Are you awake?' I called to her from my bed at the other side of the room.

'Yes,' she replied in a very soft voice.

'Did you sleep well?' I asked.

'Yes, a bit. Did you?' she asked in the same tone of voice.

Devi's mind seemed to have matured a bit during the night. 'What do you think of uncle?' she asked.

'I think he's a very sad person,' I replied.

'I know, but I don't want to leave you, especially when mum and dad aren't here,' she said.

'I know, Devi. When auntie dies, we'll be more sad.'

'So, you want me to go as well?'

'Not really, but I'm sure those people will bring you to visit me regularly. You can start school and grow up to be a good girl. I'll continue with school if I can. Who knows. I'll call you back when I grow up and get a good job. I'm sure uncle and I can learn to live,' I said, trying to reassure her.

'I still don't want to go. I want to see us grow up together. But I'm only concerned about Koosh and Parm. They don't like me.'

We were kids but we seemed to know what we were talking about. I was surprised at the way Devi talked and that she resented being adopted. She had just about come to accept that a person does not come back when they die. When mum and dad died, she always used to say that they could come back, until she finally realised that they wouldn't. Now she was being adopted, she was not so much concerned about the adoption but the separation.

My concern was uncle's decision. He had not told us whether or not he was going ahead with the plan when he had come to see us the first time. I was of the opinion that he would tell us before he finalised any decision so that I would be prepared for any surprises. Even if I had known, I could not have stopped it. Now I was not sure of my own mind. I thought of uncle's problems and so I wanted Devi to be adopted, for her own interests, and to be able to visit her regularly. I also thought that Devi was my sister and that uncle was

14

staying on our property, which meant that we had the right to stay together, but we couldn't control our destiny. That morning I was reluctant to go to school. Then I thought I would talk things over with Devi in the evening.

The day was uneventful. I had a good day and was pleased with the wonderful lessons I had. I came home at four, eager to tell Devi about the day. I put my satchel in the usual corner and . . .

'Devi,' I called out. 'Devi. Devi-i-i, where are you?'

I couldn't find Devi anywhere. I called out again . . . 'Devi. Come out. Stop playing hide-and-seek.'

I looked for her everywhere, even under the bed. There was no sign of her. Probably she's gone shopping with uncle and auntie, I consoled myself.

It was getting late and there was still no sign of Devi. I went to see if uncle was back. Uncle lived with his family in the large three-bedroom house which was adjacent to mine – a two-bedroom thatched house.

'Oh! Prem! You're here. I was about to come to see you. I was going to tell you that Devi has gone to her new place.'

At least he could have told me earlier instead of me worrying about her the whole afternoon, I thought to myself. I still couldn't say anything to any one of them because it was not considered ethical to confront one's elders.

'I'm sorry I didn't tell you before, but you would have got worried.'

I could have hated him for that, but I realised that I was still a child and needed all his help to get on with life.

'She wasn't willing to go. She needed a lot of persuasion. She cried a lot.'

I was dumbfounded by the news and couldn't cry. It

15

was as if all my tears had dried up from all the crying I did the previous night, nor could I show any emotion. If I could have, I would have run away. I thought that Devi would contact me and might need my support. I stood there hoping for the earth to open up and swallow me and make me disappear forever.

I was surprised to learn that there was no message for me from any of the people adopting Devi. There was no address where I could contact Devi either. 'By the way, Devi said she'll contact you later and not to worry too much.'

Auntie didn't say much. I felt sorry for her because she looked pale and sickly, but, due to my anger at losing Devi, I felt hatred for her for pressurising uncle to have Devi adopted. If it wasn't for uncle's talk the previous night, I would have said something which I would have probably regretted later. My world was coming apart. At first, I had had a sister to turn to, despite her naivety, and now I had no one, although uncle reiterated I should regard him as my own father. This meant that I had to bottle up pressures until I could release them to Devi when I met her. But lots of things could happen which I might forget when I saw her. She was the only close family tie I had and nobody else could replace her.

I am sure Koosh and Parm are happy now, I said to myself.

At that moment Koosh came to me and said, 'Prem, we're sorry. We'll miss Devi. I know that we've not been nice to her. Now we realise what she meant to us. When we see her next time, I promise that we'll apologise to her for our past behaviour and be nice to her . . .'

I didn't let Koosh complete her sentence before I ran off to my room. I couldn't make out whether she was being hypocritical or really realised that she and Parm had been bad to Devi and were genuinely apologising. I thought only time would tell.

I didn't bother to eat anything, although auntie came to urge me to have my supper. They let me sleep. I cried myself to sleep, oblivious of the time. I must have gone into a long deep sleep because, when I woke up, the sun was already high and uncle was by my side, calling.

'Good morning, uncle.'

'Good morning, son. It is already seven o'clock and you're still in bed. You should get up to go to school. I know you've been crying a lot because I can see your eyes are red. I've talked to you about the adoption, but you're still too young to understand all this. I realise Devi is also young, but I know for sure that she'll be grateful for what I've done. You're a boy who will grow up to be a responsible man. You should learn to fight the odds and face life as a man. You should go to school and study hard and pass your examinations. You can, if you want to, get a good job and then have a family of your own. Look at me. As I told you, your auntie is dying. Do you think I'm happy? I've learned to face life as it comes. Your cousins Koosh and Parm will grow up, get married and go away. There'll only be you and me left here. So please try to be a good boy and go to school. If you don't want to go today, it's all right. You can stay in and go tomorrow if you like.'

I saw there was some sense in his words.

'No uncle, I'll go to school today.'

'Good boy. Don't forget to have your breakfast.'

I got ready in a jiffy, had my breakfast and I was on my way to school. I was a bit late and tried to run. Running after breakfast was not that easy yet I managed to run part of the way. Before I left, I was surprised to see auntie and the cousins there to wave me a good day.

I had tried not to miss any days at school since that time, for the fear of being stuck with my uncle and the others, and at school, I could at least talk to my teacher and friends instead of staying at home and feeling lonely and sorry for myself. Every time I was at home, I was yearning to meet Devi and talk to her. The days were like silent suffering. Sometimes I would go to the nearby river, sit on a rock by the bank and, dangling my feet in the water, listen to the soothing noise of water falling from tiny rocks in mini cascades. Sometimes I used to remember how slow the pace of life had been. My father had a lot of bananas and pawpaws in the field. I could recall that bus drivers and conductors used to leave their buses at the top of the road with the passengers, walk to our place, and take the fruit that was already picked. Now that my father was gone, we didn't see any of those people.

Days passed by, yet there was no sign of Devi. There was no letter from her foster parents, and I knew Devi could not write. There were no telephones in those days, so we could not ring each other up. Years drifted by and the more I grew up, the more it seemed that the chance of being reunited was becoming impossible.

My auntie died two years after Devi had left. Uncle was devastated yet he learned to live for the sake of Koosh and Parm. Eleven years went by, then uncle married off his daughters. Now I realised that Devi must have grown up and adapted to her new home and 'family'.

I went to secondary school which was about five miles away. I used to take a bus which took me 20 minutes. I didn't do well with my examinations, partly because I

18

was always thinking of Devi and hoping that she would come to visit me one day, and partly because I had to help uncle on the farm most of the time. I was 19 years old when I left school. I was eager to look for a job. This was the time that I went for my interview and was accepted for the road-mending job.

2

My First Job

When I was accepted for the road-mending job, I was
so elated that I couldn't wait to get started. I was
checking the post quite regularly for the details promised by Mr Tate. The postman never used to deliver our
letters at home because our house was in the middle of
nowhere and about two miles from the nearest village,
and the roads were grassy and, when it rained, muddy.
So, they preferred to leave our letters at the shop in the
village called Barlow, where we used to do our shopping. We used to collect our letters once a week when
we were doing our shopping. But, because I was expecting my letter, I was there virtually every day. The day I
got my letter about the job, I ran home to tell uncle all
about it.

'I got the letter I was expecting, uncle. I'm going to
start on Monday. I've five days to get ready for it.'

'Are you sure you want the job? It may be too hard
for you.'

'I think I'll grow to like it, uncle.'

'I can see you're very happy about it. I hope you'll
enjoy yourself. May I wish you a prosperous future with
the job? Who knows, you may get promoted to a
supervisor one day. Or you may get another job later.
This is only the start of something, and probably a
lonely life for you. I'll miss you not being around to

help me, but I may get a helper. I wish Devi was here to see you off to start a new life.'

The reminder of Devi saddened me a bit, but I was soon all right after my uncle continued our talk.

'She must have grown up by now and got married.'

'Yes, uncle. No one got in touch with us!'

'I know. This is what adoption is all about. No one is supposed to get in touch. Once someone is adopted, they belong to a different family.'

'I hope I'll meet her one day and we'll be able to recognise each other. It's very hard to recognise someone when they have grown up,' I said with determination.

'Yes, I know. Anyway, son, I wish you good luck with your new and first job.'

'Thank you, uncle. The pay is not bad. I hope it won't be hard work to earn that money.'

I spent the rest of the week thinking about the job and about prospective colleagues. I knew, for some reason, that I was going to have a good relationship with them and that I would enjoy the work. I've always thought that it's not the work that is difficult. It's being with co-workers that makes it easy or difficult.

It was 5.30 on Monday morning when I bid good day to uncle and went by the main road to wait for a truck to pick me up at six o'clock. I was early because I was so eager to start my first ever job away from home. Waiting for 30 minutes was like waiting for hours. I was pacing up and down the road hoping that I would be picked up. The truck was late coming. Then all sorts of ideas ran through my mind. I was wondering if the driver had forgotten to pick me up or if I was waiting at the right place. I was thinking if the lorry arrived, I would be late for work and I might be told off for being late the first day. I was also wondering what would happen if the lorry didn't arrive at all. I would never be able to get a job and my dream would be shattered. Finally, the truck arrived at 6.20. I gave a sigh of relief. It was late because, I was told later, most of the workers weren't ready on time to set off to work. The back part of the lorry was covered with canvas – a replica of a larger version of an army jeep. The driver knew that I was the one he was picking up because I was the only one around.

'You must be Prem!'

'Oh yes, I'm Prem.'

'Hop on at the back.'

I climbed in at the back by means of makeshift steps. There were 15 workers already seated. I was the last one to be picked up. Being in a crowded area for the first time in my life made me nervous, but this nervousness was soon evaporated by the nice welcome I had. I had thought that I would be lonely and the journey would be boring and tedious because I did not know any of the people. I was wrong. The people were friendlier than I had thought. They made me feel at home and no sooner had I got in than I started talking to them as if I had known them for a long time. Some were cracking jokes and others were talking about past experiences and yet others were talking about recent films they had seen. There was no talk about television programmes because there was no television in those days.

I can vividly recall two jokes. The first one was told by Dhan (short for Dhanilall), who said that his brother had held a hen with one hand while slapping it with the other. He liked the noise it was making. The more noise the hen made, the harder his brother hit it, until the noise stopped and the hen was dead. I did not take it as a joke but it got stuck in my mind. The second joke was told by Raj. He was saying that one day his parents were out and he and his younger brother decided to bake some cakes. He had seen his mother baking but he forgot the right ingredients. Besides, the oil in which he was going to fry the cake was not hot. When he put the hand-rolled paste in the oil, it spread instead of staying in one piece. He panicked but didn't want to throw it out for his mum to find. They drank the oil with the mixture.

How revolting! I thought.

I started talking to one person called Dev. He became my best friend later.

'Tell me about the place where we're going to work,' I asked him.

'Oh! Rose Belle is a nice village. People welcome you. They're very friendly. You'll like it there,' Dev replied.

'How's the work we're going to do?' I asked him.

'It's a bit hard, but I'm sure you're going to like it as well. You'll see. I was a newcomer like you a month ago. Now I have grown to like it because these people here are very good. They help you whenever you need it. The foreman is kind and helpful as well.'

'What will we be doing?'

'Well, at present we've started constructing this new road which will run at the side of the village. We started only a few days ago. I reckon we're going to be there for the next six months.'

'How do you like the pay?'

'Oh! That's all right. It's enough to buy your ration and have enough to save monthly.'

(Ration is the term applied to food purchased in a shop. I believe the term is carried over from the Second World War. Most of the foodstuff, such as grain, is weighed on scales.)

I found that I could talk to Dev and confide in him.

23

I learned that he was 22 years old – three years older than me – but we seemed to be thinking on the same wavelength.

We had been travelling through winding roads and were going up a mountain when someone called Toon said, 'This is Nicolière. Have you been here before, Prem.'

'No. I haven't. I could see the mountain from where I live but I've never been here.'

This mountain has a lake at the bottom and it looked really nice from the top. The scenery was fabulous.

'Heeere we are,' shouted the driver.

'We've to get down,' said Dev. 'Lall, the foreman, will tell us what to do.'

'So this is Rose Belle. Is this where we'll be stuck for the next few months?' I asked.

'That's right,' replied Dev.

'I think I'm going to like it,' I exclaimed.

So this was the spot that was to be my first ever workplace. When the driver said we had reached our destination, my heart gave a thump and my stomach churned a bit but I was soon relaxed.

We had been travelling for an hour through winding roads which were bumpy in places owing to potholes and ramps. Rose Belle is a tiny village in the south of Mauritius. The place where we got off was about three-quarters of a mile to the south of the village. There were heaps of gravel and sand and drums of coal tar by a hut, where a security guard lodged during the night to keep an eye on the materials.

'So you're Prem,' said a tall slim-built person probably in his thirties. 'I'm Lall, the foreman. I know you're new. Don't worry, you'll get on all right. After you've changed into your working gear, I'll ask you to work with Dev since you seem to be getting on well together. He'll tell you what to do. But, first of all, we'll have a cup of tea. By the way, you can call me Lall.'

'Yes, Lall,' I said hesitantly because, in those days, when someone was older than us we never used to call them by their names. It was appropriate to call them brother or uncle.

When Lall was talking to me, one of the men was boiling water in a large urn on a hearth made of three stones. I was feeling peckish and I scoffed a banana which I had in my workbag. I did not have a personal cup for the tea and I had to share one of theirs for the day. The first outdoor tea was not so pleasant, but I had to drink it in order not to offend anyone. It was eight o'clock when we started to work.

'You can use this spade, Prem. We're going to dig the side of the road so that we can lay gravel on it. I know it's going to be hard for you at first. But, as I said before, you're going to like it,' said Dev.

Oh God! What have I let myself in for, I said to myself. I remembered that I had said to my uncle that I had to learn to support myself. I thought of my late parents and also of Devi.

'Yes Dev, I'm going to like it.' I thought of the coincidence of names. My sister was Devi and now I was working with someone called Dev.

It didn't take me long to get used to the job of digging because I was used to it on the farm. The only difference was that, whereas on the farm I was digging whenever I wanted, here I had to do it as a job. We were digging and throwing the soil on the side. One person was using a pneumatic drill, the noise of which pierced my ears. I supposed that others were used to such noise because no one apart from the operator was using ear muffs. Some people joked while digging in order not to feel the hard work. Everyone seemed to know what they were doing.

I had hardly dug a few feet when sweat was pouring out of me. At home I would have either had a rest or avoided working during the day when it was sunny and hot and worked early morning or in the evening when it was cool. Here I had to bear it and keep on working. I was slowing down a bit when Dev reassured me not to worry about the quantity of the work and so did Lall. Then I wanted to go to the toilet.

'Do you see the cabin over there? It's our toilet. You can use it,' Dev told me.

The toilet was about six feet long and five feet wide made with corrugated iron sheets. These sheets conducted heat and inside it was more intensely hot than it was outside. To be inside the cabin was just like being in an oven. I was soaked to the skin with sweat after being in there for three minutes.

'You're hot,' said Dev to me. 'You see, we usually start our work at seven so that we do very little when it heats up later. It being Monday, most people weren't ready, although Alan, our driver, was on time to pick us up. I hope we'll be on time tomorrow. Don't worry, we'll soon go to do some shopping for all of us. What happens is that they ask the youngest one of the team to do the shopping. So, because I was the youngest at the time, I've been buying the stuff. They all give me a list of things to buy and, when I come back, the carrier bag is full. I think it's fun joining the colleagues at lunch.'

'I've brought some packed lunch today, but tomorrow I won't bring anything so that I . . .'

'Dev,' called out Lall. 'It's ten o'clock. You'd better go to the shop and buy some food for us. Here are the lists from each one of us. Get some extra bread rolls for Prem. You may take him with you.'

It took us about ten minutes to walk to the grocery. We met the shopkeeper, who was of Chinese origin and probably in his forties.

'Hello, Dev. How are you today? Did you have a nice weekend?'

'Good morning, Mr Cheung. How are you? As for me, I'm fine, thank you. Yes I had a nice weekend, but it's a pity to come back to work.'

'You say that every Monday, Dev, don't you?' replied Mr Cheung jokingly.

'I know. Anyway, this is our new friend, Prem.'

Mr Cheung greeted me and shook hands. Then Dev went through the lists, telling Mr Cheung what he wanted. It was not a self-service shop and Mr Cheung had to serve. (We had to address Mr Cheung as such instead of by his first name because of the traditional respect for older people. We did not know his first name and there was no need for that.) Mr Cheung finished serving and gave us the bill, after doing the sum on his abacus, which was common among Chinese shopkeepers in those days. He also wrote the prices with the total in a small note book Dev had carried with him. After Dev made the payment, Mr Cheung gave me a piece of home-made cake as a token of welcome to his shop. I shared the cake with Dev on the way back.

'Mr Cheung is a nice person,' I said.

'Yes, he's a very nice man.'

It was still early for lunch, so we resumed our work. This time, in addition to digging, we had to fill wheelbarrows with gravel and transport them to areas we had dug, then fill and level the ditches. Pickaxes and spades were adding to the noise of the powerful pneumatic drill, now being operated by a different person. I had

27

never used a drill before but, I supposed, I might use it one of these days. Everyone was toiling away. Some had stripped themselves to the waist and almost everyone was in their shorts. Soon we heard a nearby church bell striking 12 o'clock.

'We break in thirty minutes for our lunch,' called out Lall. 'Jay, you can start preparing the meal for us,' he added.

The 30 minutes dragged on because I wanted to have a rest and I could also feel my stomach grumbling with hunger.

'We'll take a break now. We start back at two, all right?'

Jay had already prepared some meals from what we had bought at the shop earlier. I felt bad for not eating with the team and having to eat separately.

'Enjoy your meal, Prem,' said Raj, one of the team members.

I had learned some names already, although knowing what 15 people were called in a short time was not easy, especially when I was not used to learning names.

'Thank you! I wish I could join you. Never mind! I'll join you tomorrow.'

After lunch, some went for a stroll in the village. Others lay down under trees to rest. I also preferred to lie down and have a rest until it was time to resume work. We had visits from boys at the local secondary school. They came to see how we were progressing with our work. I fell asleep and was awakened at 1.45 by Dev.

'My God, Prem! You snore quite loudly, don't you?'

'I wouldn't know. No one has ever told me that I snore. I must have gone into a deep sleep.'

'You must have. I know you may be tired. Anyway, it's nearly time to go back to work. I thought I'd wake you up so that you can freshen yourself before we start again.'

'Oh, thanks! Oh no. I wished I could have slept longer. My body is stiff.'

'You'll soon loosen up.'

'Come on, boys,' called out Lall. 'It's time to start work.'

We resumed work at 2.10 and continued with what we were doing in the morning. The afternoon sun was more scorching than in the morning. Nonetheless, we had to work until four, when we had a wash by a fountain which was erected especially for us. We got ready and the lorry came to take us back and drop us at our individual homes.

The first day appeared to have gone quickly. It was probably because I was busy doing my work and didn't have much time to think about anything else. Everyone seemed to be exhausted because of the heat and wanted to go home after a hard day. I felt sorry for the driver, who couldn't go home until he had dropped the last person. I supposed one consolation for him was that he didn't have to work with us. His main task was to transport materials, such as cement and sand, from one place to another with an assistant. I supposed driving itself was tiring and, in that respect, he would have preferred to stay with us.

'I could be Alan's assistant,' I remembered saying to Dev.

'Sam is quite happy doing his job. Besides, I don't think you'd like that job. I think you'll be happy with us,' Dev was quick to reply.

'Ah well! I thought I would ask you,' I said.

I was home by 5.30 as I was the first one to be dropped off.

29

'How was your first day at work?' uncle asked.

'It was hard work, but I'm sure I can get used to it. At least I'm employed now and expect a wage at the end of the week, although working on the farm was fun. I think I can do with a rub-down though. Never mind, how was your day, uncle?'

'It was all right. I managed to get the work done. If it becomes too much, I might have to get someone to help me. Let's hope that won't be necessary.'

Work was similar for the rest of the time. I received my first wages in cash at the end of the second week because they kept one week's pay in hand. I was quite pleased with it. I gave part of it to uncle for safekeeping because saving in banks was not common unless one went to the city to open an account. I kept the rest for expenses at work, such as buying food for lunch as I had stopped taking packed lunches. Another change that took place was that, as Dev had warned me and because I was the youngest of the team, I was asked to do the shopping.

Two weeks had elapsed since I had started going to the shop. Then something strange happened. On the way to the shop, I used to go past a village hall and, on Mondays, Wednesdays and Fridays, some girls used to go to the hall to learn to sew, a course run by a seamstress. During one of my errands, I caught sight of two particular girls who were coming out of the hall and always seemed to be together. I suddenly was attracted to one of the two girls as if lightning had struck me. It seemed to me I had fallen in love with her. I had never felt like this before. I thought that the girl was for me and I would do anything to get her. I knew it was a hard job. In Mauritius, if a man fancied a girl, he couldn't go to the girl and ask her out. If he did that, he would either get a slap on the face or be struck on the head with her shoe. It was also a custom that, if a man fancied a girl, he had to talk to his parents and the parents, not him, would go to meet the parents of the girl. Then the girl's parents would inquire about the man's status and the parents' background before they would consider a relationship. I knew I would have to fight a losing battle if I followed the custom, because of my job, and decided to try my luck alone.

The girl was of medium build and had a fair complexion with a perfect round face. She had shoulder-length hair and might still be in her teens. Her friend looked at me and smiled. It should have been the other one to smile, the one I fancied, I thought.

I followed the two girls in order to see where they lived. I found out that they were neighbours and lived at the other side of the village, which meant that they had to walk for about ten minutes to come to the hall. They looked rich from the way they were dressed. Both lived in bungalows with large gardens in the front. Both knew that I was following them because the other girl looked back a few times and smiled. I was wondering if she was the one who fancied me. Anyway, I was confronted with the problem of approaching them. In the end, I decided to leave things for the next time because it was getting late to go back to work. I hurried with the shopping and ran back to work. I was about ten minutes late. I thought that I had to be careful if I wanted to continue with my errands.

'You're late back. What happened?' Dev asked as if he was the only one who could communicate with me. 'You look dazed. Are you all right?'

'Yes, I'm all right, thanks.'

That afternoon I kept on thinking about the girl I fancied and how desperate I was to talk to her. My mind was already in a turmoil. One might say that I was crazy, but that was the way I felt at that time. It was stupid to be in that situation, especially as I didn't know the girl and that was the first time I had set eyes on her.

'Are you sure you are all right, Prem? It looks as if you're not too well. Come on, you can talk to me,' Dev said on the way back home that afternoon.

'It's this girl I saw this morning.'

'I knew it was something like that. I read your mind the moment you came back, and everyone noticed the difference in you during the afternoon.

'Did they? I feel bad about it now you've told me.'

'Don't be. They understand. They didn't say anything to you. They told me because they know you talk things over with me. Tell me what happened, then.'

I told Dev all about that morning and how I was determined to win that girl.

'Yes but you've to be careful. You hardly know her,' Dev said.

'I know,' I replied.

3

Looking for Love

I continued with my errands as usual and continued to follow the two girls without any luck in starting a conversation with them. Then one day I said to myself, Stop being a girlie, Prem. Go and talk to them.

That morning I plucked up the courage to do it.

'Goo-good mo-morning. My na-name is P-Prem . . . I would like to speak with you if you would. I-I s-see you are learning to sew.'

I was surprised that I stuttered a bit without realising it. I was soon all right. I didn't get any response from the girl I fancied, but I was surprised the friend answered.

'I'm Seema and this is Amla. We've seen you a few times. You don't live here.'

The speech was so soft that I could barely hear her.

'No, I travel to work here.'

The girl talked to me and they kept on walking.

'Yes, we're learning to sew, and embroider as well. Our parents say that sewing is a good hobby.'

'I see. You start very early, don't you?'

'Yes at 9 a.m. until 10.30.'

When they reached their homes, they just left without saying goodbye. They appeared shy. I thought there would be another day to continue the conversation. I raced back after my shopping and told Dev about my feat with a grin on my face like a cat that had caught its prey.

'You seem to be getting somewhere. Better luck for the next time.'

'Thanks, Dev.'

My uncle noticed something different in me, but he neither asked me nor did I say anything to him. I preferred to let nature take its course. Should he ask me what was wrong with me, I would say that I was tired because, being a youngster, I would not be able to tell him about my meetings. He might ask me to leave the job because it was too tiring for me or he might know the difference between being tired and being in love. In fact, he never asked me anything, probably because he knew that, if he asked me to leave the job, he would get the same answer – I liked it. I tried to act my usual self, and sometimes when I failed to do so, he would make some comments, such as I should rest myself.

I followed the girls a few more times. On occasions Amla – my fancy – talked to me and her voice was soft and melodious. I wished the conversations were longer. Besides, my time was limited and so was theirs. I was pleased to receive some response, and every time we met, I seemed to be making some progress. I was so overjoyed with these responses that I kept Dev informed of them in case he could help me in any way.

We were progressing with our work and I was hoping that the work wouldn't come to an end before anything positive developed between Amla and myself.

'It's a pity that you're not around in the evenings. We usually come to the hall for Hindi classes at 5.30,' Seema told me.

I didn't know how to take that news. I was surprised and it made me yearn to look for a place so that I would be able to see Amla in the evening as well. I asked Mr Cheung if he knew someone who had a room to rent. I told him that I was getting tired travelling every day and that I would like to live locally in order to be able to come to work fresh every morning.

'Coincidentally,' he said, 'I've a spare room in my house in the next village which you can have. You can have a look at it and see how you like it and then decide what you want to pay for it. I'd expect you to keep it clean.'

I was thrilled with the idea that I would be able to live near the one I loved. I realised that it would be the first time that I would be living away from home on my own. It would be tough. I would have to convince uncle that I could manage on my own.

'Thank you for the offer. I've got to talk to my parents and my colleagues, and I'll let you know of my decision in a few days.'

I had not told anyone that I was an orphan. Everyone thought that I was still living with my parents.

'Take your time. The room will always be there.'

I told Dev about my decision. He was pleased about it.

'I hope you know what you're doing. If you live here, then we won't have to go your way, and it'll be quicker than usual to come here. I don't think anyone would mind. Just tell the driver.'

When I told uncle about my decision, he appeared shocked but he said; 'I hope you know what you're doing. I'll miss you being around, but I'll get used to it.'

'I'll come home for the weekends,' I said, trying to reassure him.

'That's all right. Make sure you take some clothes with you when you go.'

35

On the following day I told Mr Cheung that I would take the room and that I would move in the following Monday. Everyone showed signs of approval. When work on the Monday was over and my colleagues had gone, I went to see Mr Cheung at his shop, hoping that I could view the room and that I would like it. If I did not like it, I would have to stay there for the night and start travelling again.

'Jack, this is Prem. Prem, this is Jack, my only son. Prem is intending to stay at our place until the road-mending job is completed at Rose Belle. I'm going to show him the room, if you don't mind holding the fort for an hour.'

'No, dad, I don't mind. At least I can have company after school.'

'See you soon.'

It took us 15 minutes to walk to Mr Cheung's place and, I supposed, this was better than travelling an hour before work. On the way, he told me that Jack was 16 and studying at the local secondary school.

The house was a large bungalow. It had five bedrooms, one sitting room, well furnished with a beautiful 14-inch Pye radio sitting on a purpose-built table. It had one kitchen, one bathroom and one toilet. All the rooms were spacious. I didn't take many things with me beside my clothes, hoping that there would be bed linen and towels for my use.

'You see, I've only one son and so many spare rooms. You can stay as long as you like and, although I said that you can pay whatever you like, you don't have to pay anything. If you need anything, just ask my wife or Jack.'

'I like the room. I'll take it. I also like the area,' I said joyously.

The first night at the place was strange. Everything

36

was different from where I lived. I stayed in the first night in order to familiarise myself with the place. Mrs Cheung brought me some sandwiches and a cup of tea. She was a pleasant woman, much younger than her husband. She asked me about my family. I told her that I lived with my parents. I was the only son and that I had one sister. She waited for me to finish my supper, after which she bade me good night and left. That was a reminder of what my mother used to do for me. I tried not to show any emotion to her.

I told everyone, especially Dev, about the new place.

'You're lucky to get a place like that,' said Moosa, one of my colleagues, 'and to have the Cheungs to treat you like their son. There you are. Your parents have lost a son now. I bet they won't take a cent for the room.'

He was right. I offered Mr Cheung some money at the end of the week and he wouldn't take it. He said that I was like a son to him and that everyone liked me.

The day after moving to the new place, I went out to meet the girls in the evening. They were really surprised to see me about.

'Hello, Amla. Hello, Seema. How are you?'

'We're fine. But haven't you gone home? Your parents will be worried about you,' said Amla.

'Don't worry. They know I'm staying at a relative's place in the next village.'

I was wondering if Amla ever went out on her own and if Seema was her bodyguard. I was desperate to talk to her privately. To do that, I tried to find out when I could meet her without Seema being there.

'Do you both do the same course every evening?'

'No,' Amla replied. 'Seema is doing her course on Mondays, Tuesdays and Fridays. I do mine on Tuesdays, Thursdays and Fridays.'

Good, I said to myself. At least I can talk to her on Thursdays.

It was Tuesday, and to wait till Thursday evening was like waiting for a long time, although I continued to see them in the mornings. My heart was pounding waiting for Thursday evening and I was becoming nervous.

Incidentally, Dev asked me how I was getting on with the 'birds'. I told him that I was getting there slowly but surely and that I was meeting Amla on her own for the first time.

It was nearing 5.30 and I couldn't see her coming. I was becoming impatient because I was wondering what if, after all my effort, she was not coming out. Eventually she came out at 5.35. I waited for her to go a few yards from her house and then approached to talk to her. I didn't get any flowers for her because there was no florist in the area, and I didn't get any chocolates because sophisticated boxes were unheard of at that time. Besides, Mr Cheung's shop was the only shop in the village and I didn't dare go and ask for chocolates there. He would probably inquire what I was up to.

'Hello, Amla. How are you today?'

'I'm fine, thank you.'

'You're late for your course. You should've been in the class at 5.30. Won't you miss out?'

'I'm late because mum and dad were late coming back from the city. I had to prepare dinner. The teacher is very good. He'll help me to catch up with what I've lost.'

'What are you studying for, anyway?' I asked.

'I'm taking the advanced Hindi course with two goals,' she replied. 'The first is to become a teacher in the local primary school and the second one is personal and no one, except Seema, knows about it.'

'Okay, I won't ask you the second goal either. Anyway, do you know how hard I was trying to talk to you? I told my parents that I am staying around here because I was getting tired travelling every day, especially after working a long day. If I stayed here, I would be fresh for work in the morning.'

'I've to go now,' she said. 'I may speak with you later at 6.30.'

'See you then.'

I was wondering if I would wait for Amla at 6.30 or give it a miss. If I were to wait, where would I go for an hour? If I went back to my room, I might be too tired to come out again, especially when it started getting dark soon after six. If I stayed around, people might wonder what a stranger was doing here, because some villagers prefer to go for a stroll in the evening. In the end, I decided to go to my room and make every effort to come back, or else I would have to wait till the following Thursday to meet Amla on her own again. It was hard to go to the next village and come back, but I had to do it. It was 6.35 when she came out. Her teacher – I presumed it was her teacher – waved her goodbye. This sparked a tinge of jealousy in me although I didn't show it to her.

'How was your class?'

'Oh it was fine.'

'I would like to see you on your own more often or take you to the seaside or to the pictures even.'

In Mauritius the system of courting was very primitive and, in some instances, still is. It was taboo to hold hands in public unless one was married. It was definitely taboo to kiss in public, and if one kissed, people would look in amazement. The Asian custom was arranged marriage and it was a taboo to talk to girls as I was doing. Love marriages were rare. If someone found out,

39

either the father or the brother of the girl would hit the man chasing the girl, even if they had not done anything. So I was taking a big risk and taking advantage of Amla being on her own.

'Amla, have you got any brothers or sisters?' I asked.

'I don't have any sister but I have two brothers. One brother is at home and the other one has left home and we haven't seen him for some time.'

'What does your dad do? He must have a good job for you to have a big house?'

'Actually, my dad owns an estate and you can say that we're well-to-do people. Do you have any brothers or sisters?'

'I have a sister who is married now. And I don't have any brother.'

'What does your dad do?'

'He's a labourer. That's why I didn't have the chance to continue with my studies and that's why I'm doing a road-mending job.'

'I'm sorry.'

'Don't worry. That's life, I suppose.'

We were nearing Amla's home and I preferred to bid her goodbye rather than go by her house and risk being seen by her dad or brother. If we were seen together, I might lose the chance of seeing her on her own.

'See you next Thursday. But I'll still see you tomorrow morning. 'Bye.'

' 'Bye, Prem. It was nice talking to you.'

I continued to see Amla and Seema during the mornings. I met and talked about our personal interests with Amla the following Thursday, but the third Thursday two items of news from her hit me like a ton of bricks and were to change my feelings.

4

Rivalry and Confrontation

On the way to her lessons, we started our conversation as usual, but then Amla said, 'I like you, Prem. But do you remember me telling you that my teacher helped me with my work? Well, he's Anand and I've known him for over a year. I think my parents know that I like him and they've encouraged me to strengthen my relationship with him.'

'Is he the one who waves goodbye when you leave the hall?'

'Yes, Prem. I know it's a blow to you but I meant to tell you from the beginning. I think Seema likes you a lot. She talks about you and became jealous when she learned that you were meeting me.'

I let Amla talk, but I was fuming inside. I didn't know whether it was a betrayal or she said this just to see what my reaction would be.

'I've fancied you since I set my eyes on you. I left my parents just so I could see you very often,' I said coolly. 'I fancy you, not Seema.'

'We can still be friends or be like brother and sister,' Amla was quick to add.

'I've come this far and I'll try to continue with my venture until I succeed,' I said to her.

I recalled that Dev had told me to be careful. Yet I was more determined than before to win Amla's love. I waited for her at 6.30 as usual and saw the same guy waving her goodbye. I felt like going to him and throttling him. I resisted and waited to accompany and talk to her on the way back. When she came out, she went straight to this man with his bicycle.

'I suppose this is another of your boyfriends. What do you say to that?' I said in a calm voice.

'Prem, this is my brother, Bobby.'

I was so surprised that I didn't know what to say. Then he laid his bike against a tree and approached me.

'You, Prem. Would you leave my sister alone. People have been telling dad that you've been following my sister. He's angry and I told him that I was going to see you. So, would you go away and don't let me see you near her again,' the brother said in a harsh tone of voice.

'I won't leave her alone. She has agreed to take me as a friend.'

'Yes, but stop following her,' the brother said menacingly.

I didn't say much after that. I went straight to my room. Mrs Cheung met me and asked me if everything was all right. I had told the Cheungs that I would go out for a stroll most evenings. On odd occasions I would play a game of dominoes with Jack and he used to look forward to those games. Mrs Cheung asked me if I would like a drink.

'No thank you, Mrs Cheung, I'm a bit tired. I'll have an early night. Good night, Mrs Cheung.'

'Good night, son.'

That night I didn't sleep well. I kept on tossing and turning and thinking what to do. I said to myself, God, what have I done to deserve this? Where is the light at the end of the tunnel that my father used to talk about?

42

I didn't want to get into fights. I wouldn't know what to do if it became necessary to fight for my rights, if I had rights. At least Amla had taken me as a friend. I might have the chance to visit her at home and strengthen my love for her. But the problem of meeting her remained, and her relationship with Anand was an issue.

The following morning I got up as usual. I got ready, had my breakfast, wished good weekend to the Cheungs and went to work as if nothing had happened. I went to do the shopping as usual and told Mr Cheung that I would see him on Monday.

'Say hello to your parents.'

'I will, Mr Cheung.'

'Hi, Prem. How are you getting on with the chick?' asked Rashid later.

'All right, thank you,' I replied.

'Don't forget to invite us for the big day,' he teased me.

On the way home I talked to Dev about the problem I was facing.

'It's best you leave everything alone and look for someone else. There are plenty of fish in the sea.'

'Yes, I understand, Dev. But I am determined to win the love of Amla.'

'Have you told your parents about this?' Dev asked.

'No. But I'll tell them in time.'

'I've said before and, as a friend, I'll say it again. Be careful. We don't want to see you in hospital.'

'Sorry, Dev, but I'm determined to win her.'

I helped uncle as usual. We went fishing on Saturday in a nearby river because uncle said he wanted to eat prawns on Sunday before I went back to work on Monday. We caught about five prawns and cooked a prawn curry. The weekend was slow, especially when I was longing to meet Amla after last Thursday's confrontation. The week went by. I continued meeting the girls in the mornings and on Tuesday evening. When I went to meet Amla on Thursday evening, I was surprised to see her on her own.

'Hello, Amla. How are you?'

'I'm fine, thank you.'

'Where is your brother today?'

'He's working late. He's a bicycle mechanic and has a lot to finish off today. I talked to him about you and he's agreed to leave you alone. Who knows, dad might agree to invite you as a friend of mine later.'

'That's nice of you. But what about Anand?'

'I'm sorry, I can't do much about this. Because he is a teacher, everyone wants me to marry him.'

'Who's everyone?'

'My mum, my dad and some of my friends.'

'How do you feel about it?'

'You know very well that girls don't have much choice in this country.'

I could see she had taken me as a friend and had started pouring out her problems to me.

'I know. You can still tell them that you don't fancy that person. It's your life. Do you like him?' I asked.

'Well, I told you he is nice and helpful,' Amla replied. 'I haven't met him on his own so I can't form an opinion of him otherwise. Dad knows Anand's status and will arrange further talk about a wedding. I'm not ready to settle until I fulfil my ambition. But you know what dads are like.'

'Yes, you can say that again.'

The question of the wedding provoked me into some action before it became too late. I thought of confronting Anand himself. If so, I had to act quickly. The only time I could meet him was after Amla had gone home. I made the decision to meet him the same day. I

44

accompanied Amla home as usual and, without telling her anything, I went back to see Anand. I was lucky to see him walking down the road.

'Excuse me. You must be Anand.'

'Yes I am. Who are you?'

'Well, I'm a friend of Amla.'

His eyes lit up at the mention of her name.

'I wanted to talk to you about Amla.'

'What about her?'

'Well, I've wanted to tell you for some time that I fancy her. I want to get to know her and marry her,' I said.

'Let me tell you, whatever your name is – '

'Prem. My name is Prem.'

'Let me tell you, Prem, I've known that girl for some time now. She's nice and I love her and I'm going to continue loving her. Sooner or later my parents are going to meet her parents in order to arrange my marriage with her.'

I loved that girl and was determined to fight tooth and nail to get her. I didn't want to tell my uncle about the problem because he might tell people that I was an orphan, which might make matters worse than before, and Amla's parents might not like him because he was a labourer. People always tried to marry off their daughters to men who had a good job, a security of better education for their grandchildren. Here I might lose the battle because I was only a road-mender.

Anand might be hurt because, if one found out that one's girlfriend had another friend, one tended to finish the relationship with that girlfriend. Obviously, it hadn't affected me that way and I was more determined than ever. I was surprised that Anand wasn't affected either.

'I don't care what you say. I love her and I'll continue

45

to love her. So let me carry on with my life. See you. 'Bye.'

'I'm telling you, Anand, that I love her. I'm going to see her and try my best to win her hand.'

'We'll see.'

I went back to my room and all sorts of ideas kept coming to my mind. I had come so far and I didn't want my chance with Amla to slip away. I wondered what would be her reaction when I saw her the next time. Probably Anand and Amla would gang up against me and I would not be Amla's friend. At the weekend I went back to uncle and still didn't tell him about my so-called romantic encounters. I thought over the problems and tried to find solutions. Incidentally, uncle came up with an idea of his own which I thought was due to the way I was behaving.

'Prem, now you've got a job,' uncle said, 'I think it's best you get married and settle down. We can find a suitable girl for you in no time. What do you say to that?'

I supposed that I could forget my problem with Amla and let her get on with Anand. But I imagined that first love could not easily be erased from the mind. At least I could try and see what happened before making an alternative decision.

'I don't think I am ready yet, uncle. Give me a few more months and I'll tell you.'

'I just thought I would ask you in case you wanted to settle down and start your own family. I'll wait for your decision.'

'Thank you, uncle.'

I went back to work on Monday and carried on with the routine as usual. I met Seema and Amla on Monday and Wednesday mornings with the usual greetings and conversation. I met Amla on Thursday and I was sur-

46

prised that she didn't mention anything about my meeting with Anand. I was wondering if Anand had decided to call it a day. This meant that I still had a chance to talk to Amla. If Anand had chosen this option, then Amla would suspect something was happening. Anand might not have told Amla about our meeting because she might get worried. I was also surprised to see that Anand waved Amla goodbye and gave me a funny look.

I must stop this going-on soon, I said to myself.

When Amla came out, she said that her parents had agreed to invite me for tea one evening on a friendly basis.

Was something brewing? I wondered. Or was it a set-up? It may be that my plan was working. These and many more ideas kept coming to my mind. In fact, I was surprised that things were developing so quickly.

'That's good of them. I can come on Monday at five, if it's all right with you.'

'Oh yes. It's no problem. We'll see you before I go for my evening class.'

This was another decision-making time. I wanted to see Anand. I wondered whether it was wise to do so or wait and see what came out of the meeting. In the end, I decided to meet him. Again I was lucky. Or probably he was expecting me.

'I see you're still following Amla.'

'Yes, but I love her.'

'How can you love her when you hardly know her or she you?'

'That's my business.'

'I know. I think we'll come to mutual agreement that you leave her alone.'

'No, Anand, you can't tell me what to do or what not to do. I'll fight on.'

'Please, don't make matters worse for yourself.'

'I'm not making matters worse. It's you who are spoiling my relationship. You should leave her alone,' I said in a rather harsh tone of voice. I was astounded that I had spoken like that. It was the first time I had thought of our sizes. He was slim and tall, about 6 feet, and I was 5 feet 4 inches and medium build. I don't know who was scared of whom because neither of us would do anything other than talking.

'I'm not leaving her alone.'

'Neither am I.'

'Oh yes, you are.'

I was tempted to hit Anand, but I resisted because I realised that I had to meet Amla's parents on Monday. If I engaged in a fight, I might lose everything.

'I think you should leave Amla alone, Anand.'

Probably Anand was also tempted to hit me and resisted because he thought of his status as a teacher, as teachers were highly thought of in those days. In the end, we decided to leave.

Our work was progressing and, again, I hoped that it wouldn't be completed before something positive happened between Amla and myself. But the way things were developing, I thought something positive happening was very remote.

Monday came and I went to visit Amla and her family. The parents were there, but the brother wasn't back from his work. He wouldn't be back till late, I was told.

'Come in, Prem,' I was greeted by Amla's dad. 'We are expecting you. Come and sit down. This is Amla's mum. Amla told us all about you. Amla is so pleased for your visit that she has baked a cake for you.'

Entering the house was like going into a mansion although it was a bungalow. It had large rooms and they were well furnished. This was the first time I had entered a rich man's house. I didn't know how to behave, yet I remembered my code for the elders. Something struck me when I saw Amla's dad and I couldn't tell what it was. I kept on looking at him.

'Oh, that's nice. At least I can taste some cake baked by her.'

As I was saying this, Amla came in with a tray with sponge cake and a pot of tea.

'Hello, Prem. How are you? It's nice you could make it. You can try some of my home-baked cake. Hope you'll like it.'

As Amla was talking, she was slicing the cake and giving a piece to everyone on special plates and then pouring tea and serving everyone. It was the custom to boil the water in an urn and add tea when the water was still boiling. Sugar and milk were added before tea was served. No one was bothered about the sweetness of the drinks.

'The cake is nice,' I complimented her. 'My mum doesn't make cake like this.'

'I'm glad you like it.'

I had still not told anyone about my family although I was tempted to do so.

The conversation deepened when Amla's mum said, 'Amla is a nice girl and we've thought of marrying her off soon. We've one person in mind. He is a teacher and we think he likes her very much.'

This bit of information sounded like a bomb in my ears. I felt like screaming in retaliation, but I resisted. I didn't know how the rest of the evening finished. Probably they noticed a change in my attitude, as Amla's mum said, 'You look tired. You should go home and have a rest. You have to work in the morning. Do you want us to drop you at your relatives' place?'

'No, auntie. I'll be all right. I'm tired and have a

49

headache. The walk will do me good. Thanks all the same. Thank you for inviting me.'

'It's a pleasure. Do come again.'

I called her auntie because that was the customary way in Mauritius to address older women. As I was getting ready to leave, Amla's brother walked in. He just greeted us and went inside to get ready for his supper.

Then I bade them goodbye and walked back home without waiting to accompany Amla to her evening class, for which she was late. I was thinking what to do next. I was more determined than ever.

I had to wait till Thursday to meet Amla on her own although I continued to meet her and Seema as usual and tried to be nice to them as if nothing had happened. When we met on Thursday, I was astonishingly abrupt with her.

'I'm surprised that you haven't considered my relationship.'

'Prem, I told you that the choice isn't mine and that you could still be my friend. You went to see Anand and were rude to him. He didn't want to tell me, but he said he had to. How dare you do that? I think you should stop pestering me. If you see Anand again, I think I'll have to stop being friends with you altogether.'

'You can't do that, Amla.'

'Oh yes I can. You just try me. I've told you that Seema is interested in you. Why don't you go and see her parents? We'll help you.'

'I've told you that you are the one I'm interested in and not Seema. I'll meet Anand and talk to him,' I said.

'In that case, you'll have to face my brother as well.'

'We'll see.'

I didn't know where such audacity was coming from, but I was being brave. I didn't want this to reach the ears of my colleagues, nor the Cheungs, nor my uncle. I realised that I should have brought my uncle to do the talking for me, but I wouldn't know how to tell him the news. In fact, I wanted to leave everyone out of this matter.

On the following Thursday, Amla's brother was waiting for me outside the village hall. I knew we were heading for an argument.

'I told you to keep away from Amla. I thought you understood that she's interested in you as a friend, but now I learn that you're being a pest. If you continue to annoy her, I'm afraid I'll have to do something about it.'

'This is my personal matter. You've got to leave me alone and let me talk to Amla myself.'

'She's my sister. I won't let you talk to her if you pester her. Why don't you buzz off.'

'I won't until I talk to Amla.'

At this point I decided to walk away and talk to Anand after the class.

'Anand,' I said, 'why don't you leave Amla alone?'

'I won't, mate.' I could see he was annoyed as well. 'I've already talked to her parents about my relationship with her and they have consented to marry her off to me.'

'You can't marry her. I'll try my best to win her,' I said quite boldly.

'Look! Leave us alone and let us get on with our lives,' Anand retorted.

'Do you think it's that easy?' I didn't know whether to continue arguing with Anand or leave and think of some plans. In the end, I decided to leave and go for a short walk before going back to my room.

The next morning I went to work and carried on as if nothing had happened.

'Give my regards to Mr Cheung,' said Dev. 'Tell him that I'll catch up with him sometime.'

'Yes I will.'

That morning Amla refused to talk to me although Seema spoke to me. I was waiting for next Thursday when I could see Amla on her own. Thursday came but Amla still refused to talk to me and so did Anand.

I spent the whole weekend pondering what step to take next. I didn't want to finish with Amla because the more the problem worsened, the more I grew fond of her. In the end, I decided that I would find a way to hide in her room in the evening and try to talk to her, provided that she didn't scream for help. Luck seemed to be on my side. I remembered Amla telling me that her parents went to the city on Thursdays and were back late, and that her brother worked late as well. So the following Thursday was a golden opportunity for me to sneak into the house when it was getting dark and hide behind a wardrobe in her room.

5

A Shocking Discovery

I was fortunate that my plan worked as expected. I went in the house through the side door. The parents were already back and were in their room. I went into Amla's room, hid behind the wardrobe which I had seen when I had visited the family and waited for her arrival from her class. She finally came in and, without any delay, started changing into her night clothes. As soon as she took her blouse off, I noticed a tattoo on her upper arm. 'Oh no-o-o!' I shouted, and ran out of the room without saying anything. I thought Amla was more shocked than me to see me there. I was so shocked that I ran to my room and buried my face in the pillow and cried.

Amla was my sister Devi. I remembered that she was tattooed when we were at the seaside with our parents when we were kids.

Oh God. Is this the light at the end of the tunnel? I thought. Amla is my sister and I didn't know it. God! How am I going to undo the problems I've created. How am I going to tell her that I am her long-lost brother Prem? Yes, the same Prem that loved her and wanted to marry her. God! Help me God.

I didn't know whether to tell anyone about my discovery or to let nature solve the problem. The next day I went to work and everyone noticed that I had red eyes.

'Didn't you sleep well,' Dean, another colleague, asked me.

'No. For some reason I couldn't sleep.'

I went to the shop and met the girls. My attitude toward Amla was different. I was wondering whether to tell her that she was my sister or just carry on as normal. I decided to leave things as they were. I managed to greet them and dash back to work with my eyes full of tears. I had to make plans to patch things up, but I couldn't do anything until the following week. I was down the whole weekend. I was wondering whether to tell uncle of my discovery or not. I remembered him telling me that, once one was adopted, one belonged to another family. So I preferred not to tell him either.

On Monday I met the girls and I wanted to speak with Amla but she still refused. As usual, Seema talked to me and I thought that I would show more interest towards her. The evening came and I didn't meet the girls, as I preferred to meet Anand.

'Anand, I want to talk to you.'

'No. I've told you to leave me alone. What were you trying to do? Were you going to rape Amla or something? You're lucky no one else saw you and she didn't tell her parents or her brother. She mentioned it only to me. So get lost.'

'No, my friend. I know I was wrong.'

'How dare you call me friend!'

'No, I mean it. I think you're the only person who can understand my feeling.'

'I know that feeling, but it's about time you left us alone. Goodbye,' Anand said harshly.

I met Anand again the next day and wanted to talk to him, with the hope that he would help to patch things up. Yet I wouldn't tell him that Amla was my sister.

'I've told you to leave us alone.'

'I know, Anand. I know I've wronged you. I hope you'll forgive me. I'll let you get on with Amla and help you wherever I can.'

Anand was surprised to see me changed. I wanted him to marry Amla because he appeared to be a nice person.

'Change of heart, and then you'll think of another way to break us. I know your trick. It's best you leave us alone,' Anand said.

'I know you won't understand, Anand.'

'What do you mean, I won't understand? I understand it very well. Just go away.'

'No, Anand. I promise that I won't break your relationship. I'll help to strengthen it. Believe you me,' I said humbly.

I thought he was surprised to hear me talk to him in such a humble tone when I had addressed him harshly previously. I noticed a glimmer of understanding in him when I said, 'I'll talk to Amla and, believe me, I'll address her nicely.'

'Don't talk to her until I talk to her, or else she may slap you for the way you behaved.'

'Thank you, Anand. Tell her that I'll see her on Thursday if she wants me to. All right?'

'I'll try my best,' Anand replied.

I was glad that things were working out, but I wasn't sure Amla would compromise. I left it to time. Every time I approached Amla, she refused to talk to me. I presumed she had lost trust in me, although I was surprised to see that Seema was still talking to me. I had not seen her brother Bobby after the last confrontation.

Anand started trusting and talking to me and becoming friendlier than Amla. He even invited me for tea at his place. Then one day he came up with some good news.

'Prem, Amla and I are getting married next month.'

I was so overjoyed that I couldn't hide my emotion. I held him and hugged him with tears in my eyes and I couldn't congratulate him enough.

'Of course, I'll invite you if no one will. You can be my best man or you can just come along with me.'

'Can I invite my parents?'

'Yes you can.'

'Good. Anand, you don't know how pleased I am for you. Let's hope we'll be all right after you get wed and that Amla accepts me.'

'I'm still surprised that once we nearly came to blows because of Amla and now you are pleased for me.'

'Well, Anand, that's destiny. That's the way we are meant to be. Oh yes, before I forget, may I invite the Cheungs as well?'

'Oh, sure you can. Anyone else?'

'I know I'm being childish, but these people are my favourites.'

Thoughts came to my mind that I would have married my own sister if it was not for that wardrobe incident. Devi was getting married and I must seize the opportunity to tell the world that she was my long-lost sister. To this effect, I must invite uncle and the Cheungs. However, I was surprised that I didn't recognise Amla's parents from the time they came to see us on the farm, although her father had reminded me of someone on my first visit to her place. It was most likely I was only a kid when I saw them and that they had changed with age.

Everyone at work noticed that I was happier than before. They thought that things were really working out with my girlfriend. Who knows, Seema could become my life partner, I thought. I told uncle that he was invited to a friend's wedding and that I would like him to come. He agreed to it.

'You'll have the chance to see where I live as well.'

I talked to the Cheungs and invited them, too. And they also agreed to come.

It was my sister who was getting married and I was thinking about a nice gift for her, although Anand told me not to worry about it.

'Just come along and you'll have dinner here.'

I talked to Mr Cheung about buying a present.

'Son,' he said, 'I'll give you something to give to your friend.'

'Thank you, Mr Cheung.'

The wedding was fixed for a Sunday at one in the afternoon. I thought that was ideal in order to enable me to travel all the way from the northern village and back.

6

The Big Wedding and the Revelation

On the wedding day, I wore the same suit I wore for my interview. It was slightly tight but it served the purpose. Uncle also wore his best suit. We were an hour early at Anand's place.

I met Mr Cheung first.

'Prem, we would like to meet your parents.'

'Mr Cheung, this is my parent. My parents died when I was still little and my uncle has looked after me ever since.'

'Prem, you kept it a secret. You should have told us.'

'No, Mr Cheung. It was best to leave it like that. Uncle, this is Mr Cheung, at whose place I live.'

'Yes, sir. Prem is such a nice boy that I've treated him as my second son. You can stay with us tonight if you see you can't travel back home.'

'No, Mr Cheung. I've to catch the lorry in the morning to come to work.'

'Don't say I didn't ask you.'

After the conversation, I took uncle to see Anand, who was getting into his wedding gear.

'Oh Prem, you came. I thought you would never come.'

'How can I not come? After all, it's my best friend who is getting married.'

'Have you had dinner yet? Have your parents come?'

'Yes. This is my parent. My parents died when I was little and my uncle has looked after me ever since.'

Anand looked at me in disbelief.

'You're joking, aren't you?'

'No, Anand.'

'Prem,' he said with emotion, 'I don't know what to say. You've been so brave that I can't help admiring your courage.'

'I've told you that it's destiny. We've got to put up with it.'

'We'll be leaving at 12.45 and I've ordered a car for your guests. You can come with me as best man. I still can't believe you!'

We left the place on time. Uncle and the Cheungs got talking and their car arrived at the wedding a bit late. I learned later that the Cheungs had taken uncle to see where I lived in case we didn't get the chance to go there after the wedding.

The wedding was being held in the village hall, which was full of guests from both sides. The custom was that all the guests followed the groom in cars in a procession called *baaraat*. When the procession reached the bride's place, a group of people from each side proceeded step by step with the priest saying his mantras. When they met, the father of the bride hugged the father of the groom as a gesture of welcome. Then all the guests shook hands and mingled. I couldn't wait for all these functions. Usually, the wedding is held in the front garden of the bride's home, where a large tent is pitched to accommodate guests from both sides, but, because Amla's parents were rich, they preferred to hold it in the village hall.

I ran in to look at Amla. Her brother looked at me with the gesture of 'get out of here'. But he didn't say anything and I didn't take much notice of him because

59

I was Anand's guest. I was pleased to see Amla dressed all in red – as is the Indian custom. She looked stunning. Seema was also there as bridesmaid. She looked stunning as well. Anand looked magnificent in his wedding garb.

After the initial ceremony, the wedding started. The priest conducted the wedding by welcoming the guests. The ceremony lasted for 45 minutes, after which the priest delivered a speech congratulating the bride and the groom. Then the great moment came. I asked the priest if I could talk for ten minutes. I told him that it might bore some people but I would like to talk. He gave me permission. The table from where I was to deliver the speech was near the bride and groom. Before I started my speech, I was filled with emotion but I tried to contain myself. I made sure that I faced Amla when I spoke.

'Ladies and gentleman, my name is Prem. I don't think most of you know me, but you soon will. I asked the priest if I could deliver this speech. He has consented to it. I may have been a nuisance to some people, but I promise that I'll go away after this. I have two reasons for delivering this speech and I hope you will bear with me. Firstly, I would like to congratulate Anand and Amla on this auspicious day. They are my best friends and I'm very pleased that they are getting married. I pray that they will stay together and be happy forever.'

When I was saying this, I noticed that Amla was not looking at me. Probably she didn't want to hear my voice, but Anand was gesturing a thank-you message to me.

'My second reason is very important and I'll tell you this through a story. I knew a boy once whose parents died when he was little. He had a little sister who was adopted because his uncle, who had a sick wife and two daughters, could not cope. His uncle's wife died two years after the sister was adopted, and his two daughters grew up and eventually got married and went away. Destiny left the uncle and the boy, now grown up, to cope with life. The boy missed the sister so much that he wanted to find a job so that he could start life afresh and build a career for himself. In the end, he got a job that took him away from his home, thus leaving his uncle to cope on his own.

'When the boy found a job, he came across a girl and fell in love with her straight away. You could call it infatuation, but he knew that it was love. From that moment he was determined to win her love. To this effect, he had to confront her boyfriend and her brother as he couldn't bear to see her married off to someone else. What he did one day was to hide himself behind the girl's wardrobe in order to get her for himself, an action that upset the girl and her friends. Do you know what he found out? He saw a tattoo on her left upper arm that was imprinted when she was a child. Yes, the girl was his sister.'

At this moment Amla had lifted her head and I could see her looking at me with tears in her eyes.

'Yes, Amla. You are my sister Devi. Come to your brother.'

At this point, Devi got up and walked slowly to me. I also walked to her. When we met, we got into an everlasting embrace, crying like two small kids. Everyone stood up and I could feel that they were all weeping. We stood holding each other for more than ten minutes. Then I said, 'Go, sister. Anand will look after you. He's a nice person.'

In the meantime, Anand also came with tears in his eyes and thanked me for making it a great day. Amla's brother came to me and so did his parents. Amla's father said to me, 'Prem, you are not going anywhere. You're staying here. You're welcome at our place any time you like. Consider us as your parents. We know that this is the best present Amla has received for her wedding, her brother. Her happiness is your happiness.'

Uncle came and he could hardly speak. It was at this moment that Devi saw uncle. She got in an embrace with him, and cried.

The Cheungs came to me as well, in tears. Mr Cheung said, 'I've attended many weddings, but I've never seen such an emotional one. You are great, my son. From now on I'll ask you to address us as uncle and auntie instead of Mr or Mrs Cheung.'

It was Devi's wedding day, but she preferred to spend most of the time with me, talking about the lost days and forgetting that uncle and I had to go back home. We asked leave from Anand, Devi and her parents, and also from the Cheungs.

We caught the bus to the city and managed to get the last bus from the city to reach home at six in the evening.

'God, you were brave. What a coincidence to get a job where, unknown to you or to me, Devi lived!'

'Yes, uncle. God helped me. I had a feeling that I would find Devi some day.'

'I was surprised that you kept everything bottled up until the right time.'

'I had to, uncle. I've learned that we've to be sure of something before we act, just in case we're disappointed in our endeavour. You see, if I had told you about Amla, you would have advised me adversely and I might not have been lucky enough to find my sister.'

'You're right there. Anyway, I am glad that you're

happy now. We can inform Koosh and Parm about your feat and invite them for a family reunion. I'm sure Devi would like to come along. What are you going to do now that you've found your sister? Are you going to continue with your job?'

'Yes, uncle. I know things will be different, but I'll carry on as usual.'

'Mr Cheung is nice. He showed me your room and I'm glad that you live there. It will be a pity when your work finishes in that area. Then you might have to find ways to go back to visit the people there.'

'Uncle, we've got to leave things and see how they develop. What I want to do right now is to go to sleep. We had a long day.'

'Sure we had. See you in the morning, Prem.'

7

New Horizons

I didn't sleep well that night. I was pondering uncle's statement about being brave in order to face Devi's step-brother and Anand. I wondered why I was worried. I had already found my long-lost sister. I should be happy. I was also thinking that I took up the road-mending job because I had wanted to go out and meet people. The thought of Devi had been at the back of my mind. I wondered if I would still have the same enthusiasm to work. It was then that I began thinking of the farm. I had toiled there most of the time. I was also thinking that, if I decided to leave the job, I would miss my colleagues, who had shared my problems when I needed them. Dev came to mind. He had been a special friend and an advisor. Mr Cheung had been like a father to me. Above all, now I had to look forward to seeing Devi. With this last thought, I decided to continue with my work.

I got ready on Monday morning and waited for the lorry. It was a new me who was going to work, and my colleagues saw a difference in me. I thought that I would continue with my revelations.

'You look happier than usual. I think you've struck the right chord with your girl,' commented Dev.

I managed to narrate the whole story during the hour's travel to the workplace.

'You mean to say that you lied to us that you were living with your parents,' Toon stated.

'Yes. I had to because I didn't want to bring my problems to work.'

'Indeed, you didn't show you had problems. We admire you for your courage. Don't you think Prem deserves a round of applause, lads?' Toon said.

At this, they all clapped and cheered. Later Alan, the driver, asked what all this cheering was about.

'Did you know that Prem doesn't have parents? They died when he was little. He lives with his uncle. To top it all, he has just found his little sister who was adopted when he was still a child,' said Ram.

'You're brave, man,' Alan said.

Lall was also pleased to see me happy. I carried on with my work as usual. I went to the shop and was greeted by Mr Cheung with a big hug.

'Prem,' he said, 'we couldn't stop talking about you last night. I am glad you came to work.'

'No, uncle, I've got to work.' I remembered he had asked me to address him by uncle.

'Your auntie will prepare a nice dinner for you tonight. Make sure you don't get invited anywhere else. Okay?'

'Yes, sir.'

On the way I thought I wouldn't see Devi because she was honeymooning, but I was surprised to see her talking to Seema. As soon as she saw me, she ran to greet me. We embraced each other and both of us cried again.

'I thought you wouldn't come to see us. How are you and how is uncle?' Devi asked.

'We're fine. I thought that you weren't talking to me.'

'Ha! Ha! You know, I couldn't stop talking about you

last night. Even Anand didn't bother to stop me. Do you remember the last night we spent together? We kept on waking up and asking whether we could sleep or not? They say that people forget their childhood experience. I haven't forgotten anything except that, when we grow older, we change and we fail to recognise people we haven't seen since childhood – like we did.'

'But didn't you know my name?'

'To be honest, I've met a few people with the name Prem and, when I met you, I didn't give it a thought.'

'Would you've recognised uncle if you had seen him somewhere?'

'I don't think so. I would have by his handicap and the way he walks. I've got so much to say that I would like you to come to our place tonight.'

'Devi, you've still got relatives at your place. It's best to leave it till tomorrow. I won't hide behind the wardrobe, I promise.'

'You can hide but I'll find you out,' she said, sobbing.

At this point, Seema intervened by saying that I was very brave.

'And you didn't talk to him after that,' Seema said to Devi.

'Yes. I'm sorry. Any girl would have done that. Now I'll never stop talking to you,' Devi said.

'I've to go back to work. See you.'

The Cheungs had prepared a special Chinese meal for me that night. We sat at a round table and ate our food.

'Thank you, auntie, for preparing such a delicious meal. I really enjoyed it.'

'Not at all, son. It's a pleasure. You were marvellous yesterday. We were all touched by your courage, and to deliver such a wonderful speech! I think everyone in the hall admired you for that. It was good.'

'That's the story of my life, auntie,' I said.

I went to see Devi and Anand at their place as promised and was surprised to see that she had baked the same cake as on my first visit to her place.

'I know you liked the cake. So I've baked you another one. Do you remember saying that your mum doesn't bake cakes like that? Well, mum isn't there and I'm going to bake you more cakes that I've learned at cookery classes.'

'Mm! That will be nice.'

A few weeks had elapsed after the marriage Devi and Anand when Devi came up with some astonishing ideas.

'Prem. At first I thought you might have got married. Obviously, you haven't. Do you remember that I told you that Seema had an eye for you? Well, since we've met, she has talked to her parents and wishes to marry you. You can't say that it's me you fancy. You've got me now. What do you think of it? She's a nice girl, as you know, and I'll be glad if you marry someone I've known as long as I've been here.'

'I know I've got you,' I said. 'If that's what you want, I think it'll be all right. I've to talk to uncle about it,' I added.

'I've also been thinking about your job. Are you really keen on it? Is that what you want to do for the rest of your life? You can carry on if you are enjoying it.'

I was surprised that Devi asked me these questions, to which I replied. 'I haven't got good qualification and couldn't get a good job although I have been to several interviews. I took this job because I wanted to go out and meet people. The people I work with are nice and I like the job although it's hard work. I had wanted to go to England to follow a nursing career, but I've been prevented doing so because of shortage of money and poor qualifications. I've heard people saying that qualifications don't matter that much because, since you can speak English, they'll train you,' I explained to Devi.

'Have you talked to uncle about your ambition?'

'How can I, Devi? He can't do much about it.'

'Another thing I remembered was about Koosh and Parm. Thank God, they're married. You know how rotten they were to me? I can never forgive them for the way they treated me,' Devi said quite adamantly.

'I know, Devi. They are married and gone. I think they're willing to apologise. You're grown up and it's best to forget and forgive. Uncle is thinking of having a family reunion when he'll invite you and his two daughters. Anand will have to come along, too,' I said.

'One thing I must tell you, Prem. It's so nice to hear your manly voice and you calling me Devi as you used to.'

'It's nice to hear your voice and you calling me Prem as you used to. It's just so nice,' I replied.

I spent the next few days thinking about what Devi had suggested to me. At first I was surprised that Devi had come up with such proposals. I thought that as mum wasn't there to talk to me about these issues, probably Devi had taken her place and, besides, she had led a more sheltered life than me. With this in mind, I pondered on her ideas and decided what was best. I talked to uncle and the Cheungs about Seema – Devi's bridesmaid. They all agreed that Seema was attractive and that she would be suitable for me.

After the wedding, I stopped meeting the girls that often although both continued with their classes as usual, but going their separate ways afterwards. Devi knew when I was going to do shopping for my colleagues. A few days had elapsed since she had talked to me and, because she had not seen me, she waited for me and invited me to her place. I agreed to go the same evening.

'Have you thought about what we said last time?' she asked.

'Yes, but before I say anything, I would like to know how you have managed to remember everything that happened so many years ago. Usually children forget details of occurrences from their childhood, yet you haven't forgotten any of it,' I asked curiously.

'I made myself remember everything,' she replied. 'It wasn't easy.'

'Yet, when I told you my name was Prem, you could have remembered something,' I said.

'Yes, but do you remember I told you that I had met other people with the same name? Well, I asked them where they were from and they mentioned different places. Then, when you said you lived with your parents, I didn't bother asking you. In the end, I thought, I won't go asking everyone about where they live. I left it to God to help me.'

'Think about it. If it wasn't for your tattoo, we would never have met.'

'I know. From now on, I'm going to adore this tattoo. Do you remember me telling you that I had two reasons for doing my course and that I've a second reason that no one knows about? You said that you wouldn't ask me either. Well! I've always thought that, when I found myself a teaching job, I would save some money, search for my brother, and help him whichever way I could. I would have told Anand the truth and he would have helped me.'

At this instance, Devi became emotional, which, in turn, made me emotional. We hugged each other as we did when we were little. Devi was still sobbing when she said, 'Now I've found you, I would like to help you with your dream. Anand and I discussed you and even talked about these issues to my parents – I'll continue calling them parents because I've grown up with them. We've all decided that you should try your luck, go to England and take up your dream career – the nursing profession. My parents will help you financially.'

'I don't know what to say. I'm chuffed. I've talked to the Cheungs and even Mr Cheung has decided to help me with my fare.'

I talked to uncle about the proposals made by Devi.

'It's up to you now. Besides, she's your sister. If that's the case, then you have to start by making an application to the Ministry of Health,' uncle suggested.

'The only problem is that I don't want to leave you alone in this place. I think we'll build a house for you on the property at Belle-Vue-Maurel, where you'll have the company of the neighbours. Here you are alone, with the thought that I am here for the weekends.'

'You shouldn't worry about me, Prem.'

'No, uncle. You're not getting younger. We've got to start the project of building a house before looking for new horizons for myself abroad. Don't worry about the farm. You can employ someone to look after it or lease it to someone,' I suggested.

On Monday evening I was resting in my room when Mr Cheung came to see me. I jumped off the bed and sat on the chair next to the bed.

'How are you getting on, son?'

'I'm fine, thank you, uncle.'

'How is your uncle? I must see him. Either I should visit him or you can ask him to come to see us. What's your plan about going to England?'

I told Mr Cheung about my plan and that I wouldn't

70

start applying to go abroad until the house was built and uncle had moved into it. He told me to start applying straightaway before there was a change in the law. I was surprised when he said he would help me financially with the construction of the house. This was the first time I hugged Mr Cheung and cried.

'Take it easy, Prem. I've always considered you as my other son. I'm prepared to help you as much as I can. I know you won't let me down.'

'I don't know what to say, uncle.'

'Don't say anything. Just start applying for the job in England and start the project of building the house for your uncle,' Mr Cheung urged me.

I talked with my colleagues about my plan to go to England. They were also pleased. They advised me to take a holiday for two weeks in order to make my arrangements.

'Don't forget to write to us,' Raj said. 'We'll give you our addresses. Keep them safely.'

I couldn't believe that all these things were happening to me. It seemed to me that my worries were over. My dad was right when he told me that there was always a light at the end of the tunnel. I hoped that all the uncertainties would continue to unravel with time.

New horizons were opening. First, as planned, uncle arranged a family reunion. Koosh and Parm came with their husbands and children. Devi came with Anand, and I was surprised that Seema came with her father. I had invited the Cheungs but only Mr and Mrs Cheung came – Jack had to stay behind to look after the shop. I also thought I would invite my colleagues. Unfortunately, only Dev came with his wife.

'I didn't know you were married.'

'Ah! You never asked me.'

What a family reunion! I thought to myself. I considered these people to be part of my family because they were by my side when I needed them most.

No sooner had they come when Devi got into conversation with Koosh and Parm. As if by magic they recognised each other, or probably they guessed who they were. Koosh and Parm wanted to hug Devi but Devi was reluctant to do so.

'Come on, Devi. Please forgive us. We know we treated you badly. We didn't realise what you meant to us until after you had gone. We were rotten to you and it has played on our minds,' Koosh said.

'What do you mean you were rotten to her?' asked uncle.

'Yes, dad. Even Prem didn't tell you anything, but I think Devi was pleased to leave because of us.'

'I don't think I can tell you off now. You're grown up and realise where you went wrong. I think I'll apologise to Devi for such treatment. We've to remember that past is past and that we've got to forget and forgive.'

Uncle had hardly said these words when Devi, Koosh and Parm got into an embrace with tears streaming down their cheeks. After such an emotional encounter, Devi went round looking at the places where she had spent her childhood. I could see that tears were streaming down her cheeks. After an extensive tour, she came and hugged me and, sobbingly, said: 'Nothing has changed. You've kept the place as it was when I left.'

'I've managed to keep it that way with the help of uncle.'

Uncle and I had prepared a meal for all the guests and even pitched a large tent where we had laid chairs and tables. Devi, Koosh, Parm and Seema served the food, and, after they had finished, they were asked to join in. At this point, uncle delivered a speech thanking all the guests for their presence, although it wasn't easy to get to the place where we lived. After the speech, I was surprised that Anand got up to speak.

'I'm sorry I've got to make this speech, but I think Amla is too much affected by the visit to her old place. It's nice to be here and I, on behalf of all the guests, would like to thank Prem and uncle for all they have done to welcome us. Uncle and Uncle Om, Seema's dad, have had conversations unknown to Prem, and I would like Uncle Om himself to tell you all about it.'

I was surprised about that because, although I saw Seema's dad talking to uncle, I thought it was just ordinary talk about the place and other matters.

'Yes, I am Om. I would also like to thank Prem and his uncle for the reception they have prepared for us. I've known Prem for some time and Seema has talked about him a lot. Seema likes Prem, and her mother, who couldn't come today, and I like him too. We have, with his uncle's consent, decided that they should get engaged today to be married soon. Devi, his beloved sister, has also consented to this proposal.'

I couldn't believe what was happening. I got angry with uncle for not discussing this with me, but, when I heard about Devi accepting the proposal, I cooled down. All I could remember was that I was staring with mouth open at the speaker as if I had had an electric shock. Everyone, except Seema, stood up and clapped. I thought Seema was also shocked at such a development. I couldn't see her reaction because her head was bent. When she lifted her head, I saw tears in her eyes.

Her father continued, 'I'm sure Prem will accept this offer and we wish them both a very happy and everlasting life together.'

After this speech everyone congratulated me.

'She's a nice girl, Prem,' said Dev.

73

'I know. I wish my uncle had said something so that I could have prepared myself instead of getting the shock of my life.'

'You know what they say?' Dev said. 'Life is full of surprises. They did the same thing with me when they announced my engagement to my wife, Leela.'

Everyone left by three o'clock and uncle looked at me and said, 'I'm sorry I couldn't tell you anything because Devi was the hostess. She wanted to surprise you, as you surprised her on her wedding day. I must admit, Seema is a good partner for you. Devi knows her, and she won't let you down.'

'I know, uncle.'

The next Monday I talked to Lall about taking two weeks' leave in order start my arrangements for going to England.

'Tell me when you want them. Just give me a few days' notice.'

'Thank you for your help, Lall.'

'You're welcome.'

I wrote to the Ministry of Health about my application to go to England. I had to wait till Saturday to go to the post office, which was about three miles from where I lived and near my old secondary school, to buy a stamp and post the letter, because I was working weekdays and there was no post office in Rose Belle. I also had to wait for Saturdays to go to check for letters at the shop where we bought our ration, unless uncle went there during the week.

At last I received a letter from the Ministry of Health, saying that they wanted me to come for an interview at a week's notice in Port-Louis. I talked to Lall and showed him the letter. He told me to wait for two days and he would talk to his boss – Mr Tate.

After only a day, Lall said, 'Prem, you know you've

74

four weeks' leave. Mr Tate said that you can take two weeks now and the other two weeks later.'

'Okay, Lall. I'll have only one week next week and the rest as required, if it's not a problem with you.'

'It's all right. It's your holiday,' he replied.

'Okay, thanks.'

I was glad that my leave was approved. I talked to Devi and the Cheungs about this new development.

'Be careful, Prem,' Devi said. 'I've heard that most people who have gone abroad stopped writing letters to their families. When you go, don't forget us.'

'How can I, Devi? I did so much to look for you. Do you think I'm going to forget you? Uncle has been at my side helping and advising me. Do you think I can forget him? Mr Cheung has been like a father to me. Do you think I can forget him? All my colleagues have been nice to me. Do you think I can forget them? I'll never forget anyone because everyone is part of my life, sister.'

'I know, Prem, but I don't want to lose you again.'

'No, Devi. You won't.'

Mr Cheung told me the same thing and got a similar reply.

I went for my interview wearing my old suit. I didn't feel awkward this time because I was getting used to wearing it. Besides, it was August and it was cool. I didn't have a problem finding the place. I showed my letter to the uniformed doorman, who directed me to the right department. Then I showed my letter to the receptionist, who asked me to take a seat and she would call someone to see me.

'Mr Rey?' said a slim tall lady in mini skirt and stiletto-heeled shoes. 'My name is Miss Suman. Come this way, please.'

8

Preparations for Emigration

Miss Suman took me into a room which has several partitions. Each partition was occupied by people being interviewed. We went into one of the partitions, which had a telephone, three chairs and a round table with a file. Miss Suman told me to make myself comfortable. She would like to ask me some simple questions as a formality. I was surprised that, instead of talking to me in English, she talked to me in broken French (Creole) throughout the interview.

After asking me questions about why I was interested in the nursing profession and if I would like to come back after my training, she said, 'I'm glad to say that your application is successful. The law was changed only last month. Before, we were sending people to hospitals of our choice because most of the candidates did not have a clue about the country or the hospitals. What we do now is to give you a list of hospital names and addresses and let you choose the hospital and the areas you like. I'm giving you these addresses and, if you don't get any joy, come to us and we'll give you some more addresses. We'll give you a letter. Make some photocopies and send a copy with each application you make. Okay, Mr Rey?'

'Yes, Miss Suman.'

'When you're accepted by a hospital, get your passport, and go there by air or by sea, depending how long you've got before the training starts. All right, Mr Rey?'

'Yes, Miss Suman,' I replied again.

'Thank you for your time. Good luck with the applications. See you later. 'Bye.'

' 'Bye, Miss Suman.'

When I went outside, three people who had also been for interviews were talking and stopped and asked me, as one would do after an examination. 'Hey! How did you get on?'

'I got through the interview and now I've to write to the hospitals,' I replied.

'Why don't you go and see Moosad,' one of them said.

'Who is Moosad?' I asked.

'He acts as a middleman. He does everything for you. You give him your name and address and he'll write to you when he gets a hospital for you. He charges you for that, but it's worth it. He owns a shop in the high street in Port-Louis. You can go and see him any day you like except for Sunday.'

I took the address and left.

I was overjoyed that I had been successful with the interview. Everyone was pleased.

'What are you going to do about Seema?' uncle asked. 'We've got to tell her dad so that he won't get worried.'

'Well, uncle, it has to be either a quick wedding and leave her here to look after you and call her to England later, or come back after a year or two and get married and take her with me,' I suggested.

'I don't think you'll have much time, especially when you're busy preparing for your new career. I think you've got to promise to all the parties concerned that you'll come back to marry her.'

'I'll do that, uncle.'

This was agreed by Seema's parents, as well as by Devi.

I started writing to the hospitals that I was given by the Ministry of Health. I received some replies stating that either they had stopped recruiting people from abroad or they didn't have any vacancies. Then I thought of Mr Moosad. I talked to uncle about him and asked him if he would go along with me. He decided to go with me one Saturday. We found his shop. A tall, balding person was serving some customers. We looked around until he was free.

'How can I help you?'

'Are you Mr Moosad?'

'Yes, I am. What can I do for you?'

'We heard that you help people to find hospitals in England,' uncle said.

'Yes, I try my best.'

'My son here wants to go to England to do nursing. Can you help him?'

'Have you brought any documents with you, such as the letter from the Ministry of Health and your educational certificates?'

'Yes, I have.'

He looked at the papers and said, 'I can't see you'll have any problem. Come and see me in two weeks. It'll cost you 500 rupees. You can bring the money with you,' he said to me.

'That's all right,' uncle said, although 500 rupees was a lot of money in the late sixties.

'Where would you get 500 rupees from, uncle?' I asked when we went outside.

'Don't worry. We'll find some way.'

I was checking for letters at the shop only on Saturdays, so I was surprised that I got a letter from Mr

78

Moosad within a week asking me to go and see him as soon as I could. I got the letter in the morning and I decided to go and see him the same day. I caught a bus at 11 and found him at the counter.

'Hello, Mr Rey. I'm glad you came.'

'Sorry I haven't brought your money,' I said.

'That's all right. You can bring it next week. We've got a hospital in Southampton that deals with mentally subnormal people and requires people with qualifications like yours. If you wish, you can leave by sea on the sixth of February. That gives you two months to get ready. The French ship *Jean Laborde* is leaving on that date and it's best you make your reservation as soon as you can. I thought of your financial problem and it's cheaper than going by air. Can you do that? Talk to your dad about it. Okay? See you next week.'

I had no chance to talk to him because customers were in his shop and he went to attend to them.

I didn't have any idea about what type of hospital it was nor what 'mentally subnormal' nursing meant, but, so long as it was the nursing profession, I didn't mind. I was elated and couldn't wait to tell uncle and others this news.

When I told uncle, he said that he would help me as much as he could. It was the first time I realised that, when I left, communication with him would become rare because he couldn't read or write as he had not been to school, unless he asked someone else to write on his behalf.

I paid Mr Moosad his fee and he wished me good luck as he gave me the acceptance letter from the hospital. I managed to get a passport and a ticket for February.

The month before the departure to England, Mr Cheung, Amla's 'parents' and Seema's parents helped financially to build a two-bedroomed house at Belle-Vue-Maurel for uncle. Amla/Devi – I call her by both names sometimes – and Anand promised to pay uncle a visit every weekend. I visited Seema at her parents' place every Sunday, despite seeing her every day from work. All my colleagues gave me their addresses and told me to write, and I promised that I would never forget to write to them. I took my remaining two weeks' holiday before leaving so that I could do some shopping for myself. Uncle had decided to move to his new house after I left because I didn't want to leave the place where I had spent all my childhood.

The sixth of February came and the place was packed with friends and relatives. Seema had also come with her parents. The ship was due to leave at four in the afternoon and we had to be there two hours before in order to check in. I got my cabin number and a boarding and invitation card for maximum five people per passenger to visit the ship. After the check-in and after my luggage had gone, I met and hugged everyone and went on board. Only uncle, Seema and Devi decided to go with me to look around but had to come out half an hour before the departure. The anchor was lifted and the ship left the harbour at four o'clock.

9

Journey to the Hospital

I left everything in the cabin and went up to the top deck to wave everyone goodbye. The ship set sail and I stood on the deck, waving.

Devi and Seema were both holding uncle until the ship disappeared over the horizon.

I went back to my room. I felt sad because I was leaving uncle and Seema as well other loved ones behind. I was thinking how each one might be feeling. Devi must have felt bad because she had already experienced one separation when she was adopted. By the same token, she might not feel so bad because she had uncle and Anand there. I also felt sad because I was out in the wide world on my own. I had had uncle to advise me but now it was left up to me to make all the decisions. Besides, everything was new and, as Mr Cheung had said, I had to be careful not to mix with the 'wrong crowd'. I wasn't sure how I would know whether a crowd was right or wrong. I wouldn't know until I had reached my destination. I was also not sad because I was in the process of learning.

The first thing I found to be different was the ship. I had not realised that the ship was so large and that so many people could fit in it. Instead of unpacking my belongings and looking to see what people had given me as going-away presents, I preferred to go and look around. I almost locked myself out because I wasn't used to carrying a key for my room. Then I found some string and tied the room key along with my suitcase key and put them in my pocket. I went round admiring the upper deck with its swimming pool and the second deck with the bar, where some people had already arrived to buy drinks. I was so dazzled by the new place that I forgot where my room was. I had forgotten to make a note of its number. I asked one of the ship officials, who helped me find my room but said that it was unusual that my key didn't have a tag with the room number. He told me not to forget that my room number was 16 on the third deck.

I unpacked some of my clothes and put them in the wardrobe and some other things that I might need on the table. I found from the ship's procedure leaflet that supper was being served at seven o'clock on the second deck.

Most of the time I was served with sandwiches and fruit. At other times, I had French bread with soup. Meals like these didn't make me feel homesick.

I met several other Mauritians who were going to England to follow the nursing profession and were travelling in the fourth class and had to sleep on hammocks. I made friends with them and spent most of the time with them, talking and playing games.

We reached Reunion, an island next to Mauritius, the next evening and anchored there for two days. We were allowed to go out wherever we wanted so long as we came back at certain times for meals and at a certain time for departure. I couldn't go anywhere because, as I was allowed to have £30 as pocket money when we reached England, I only had £50. I wrote a letter to Devi telling her to send me £10 in case I needed it. Fortunately, the postage was free on the ship and I managed to send some cards back home as well as my letter.

We set sail in two days. We went around Madagascar, a large island to the east of Africa, stopping at three main harbours. Then we went to the island of Comores (north of Madagascar), where we stayed outside the harbour and didn't have the chance to visit the island, although several Comoreans joined the ship and stayed in the fourth class for the rest of the journey to Marseilles. We left for Durban along the Mozambique channel. When we were crossing this channel, the sea was rough and I became seasick. I was throwing up and could not eat anything. One of the Mauritians from the fourth class took me to see a doctor on the ship. I was asked to stay in the sick bay for at least two days, but I became bored and left the sick bay of my own accord after one day and I was told off for leaving prematurely.

I noticed that when the ship was rocking sideways, there was no bad effect on us. We could see the sea right up to our window. It was scary but I didn't feel anything. It was only when it was going in a gyrating motion that I felt sick. However, I was all right by the time we reached Durban.

In Durban, I received £10 sent by Devi. Here we were allowed to go out for a few hours. I went to exchange £5 in a a local post office and was told off for entering a 'white only' section. When I went to the other section, I was surprised to find the same person serving me. I felt like telling him that he was in a 'non-white' section, but I preferred to take my money and go. Another interesting problem I found in Durban was that buses and bus stops were clearly marked for 'whites only' and 'non-whites only'. In the city I saw rickshaws, a type of two-seater cart, pulled by Zulus, the native Africans. I was also fascinated by escalators, which I described as moving stairs when I wrote to Devi. Some native Indian girls came to visit the ship and I exchanged addresses with them and kept in touch with one of them for few years afterwards. We also managed to see some dolphins swimming in the harbour.

We left Durban and sailed to Cape Town. Although we stayed outside the harbour, we managed to see the scenery from the top deck. In front of us we could see Cape Town with tall buildings. On the right, we could see the Table Mountain with its flat top. Although it was summer in the southern hemisphere, the top of the mountain was snow-capped. When the sun rose in the morning, it was nice to see its rays glittering on the top.

After Cape Town we headed for Senegal, north-west of Africa. The ship sailed for five days along the west coast of Africa. We couldn't see land. The only thing we could see was a blue line over the horizon. It was announced on the noticeboard, where we checked daily occurrences, that we would be crossing the equator at 11 in the morning. I was excited about experiencing the equatorial heat, but I was disappointed when we crossed it because it was raining and it was cool.

We were becoming bored with seeing the vast sea for five days before we reached Dakar, the capital of Senegal, and looking forward to land. So we were disappointed when we were told that we would be there for only a few hours and that we were not allowed out. We could see Senegalese people around but not the city as we stayed in the harbour.

We left Dakar for Marseilles, in the south of France, the final destination of the ship after 35 days at sea. I packed my belongings and exchanged some addresses with some Mauritians and a Kenyan Indian teenage boy who befriended us during the voyage and who was going on holiday to France. I made sure that I had my tickets ready for the train journey from Marseilles to Paris. I, with some Mauritians, went to the station, checked for the scheduled train as indicated on our tickets, and also inquired at the train information desk, and boarded the train. Fortunately, we didn't have to buy tickets because, when we paid for our fare, everything was included until we reached our destination, the hospital.

This was the first time I had seen a passenger train. We had had trains in Mauritius, but they were discontinued before I could see them. We still had cargo trains that were used to transport sugar cane to the sugar factories.

We travelled through the night, so I didn't have much chance to see the south of France. I was surprised that we could walk about in the train. It was quiet and we managed to doze off a few times although we found it odd travelling by train the first time. We didn't make ourselves comfortable for fear that we might miss our destination.

We reached Paris and, when we asked, we were told to be quick because the train to Calais was to leave in 30 minutes. We were shown which platform to go to. The Gare du Nord was a vast station with several platforms, and we had to carry our suitcases as no one had told us to use a trolley. We managed to catch the right train, which left the station as soon as we boarded it. No sooner had it left the station than the train started running fast. I was feeling hungry and wanted to buy something to eat. I was told that I could buy something at the buffet and that I could use English money. This enabled me to use £5 to buy some sandwiches and a cup of tea.

I caught glimpses of the north of France. I couldn't see much of it because I wasn't sitting by the window.

We reached Calais and had to catch a bus to the harbour. When we got there, we were told to wait in the lounge for three hours before we could catch a ferry for Folkestone. It was a long wait because I was feeling tired and hungry, but I went to buy something to eat at a café with the change I had from the train.

We boarded the ferry from Calais to Folkestone and set sail late in the evening. The Channel crossing took about three hours. I did not feel seasick because the sea was calm and I was already used to travelling by sea. So I managed to have a few naps during the crossing.

We reached Folkestone and went through customs, and for the first time officials looked at all my papers, including my passport, the letter from the hospital which Mr Moosad had given me and the letter from the Ministry of Health. After everything was checked, an entry visa was stamped on the passport for one year, after which the hospital had to renew. The law was that the visa was renewed every year for five years by the hospital and, when I was qualified and if the hospital still wanted to employ me, I was to get a permanent visa, which meant that I would be free to go in and out of the country so long as I came back within two years. This permanent visa also meant that I wouldn't need a work permit and could be employed anywhere in the country.

We took our luggage to a bus which dropped us at the train station. The train to Victoria came at eight o'clock and left in 30 minutes. It went through Kent. On the way, we could see the countryside and a few buildings. We could not tell where we were because the train was going too fast. In the end we reached Victoria at about ten o'clock.

We came out and the other Mauritians went their separate ways. I was on my own and I felt stranded. I went and asked for the train to Southampton and was told to take any train to Clapham Junction and catch the train to Southampton from there. When I was waiting around, I heard someone buying a ticket. I thought that that person was a stranger as well because, when he asked for a ticket for Gillingham, the seller asked him 'single?' to which the man replied, 'No, I'm married and have two children.'

The seller explained, and this was a lesson for me as well, 'When we say single, we mean to say whether you want it one way, that is you're not coming back, or return, that is you are coming back.'

'Oh I see,' the man replied.

I asked for directions and made sure that I took the right train to Clapham Junction.

When I came to Clapham Junction, I had two interesting experiences. The first was that, when I asked one man about the direction to the platform for Southampton as Clapham Junction was large, he didn't bother to talk to me and kept on walking. When I asked another person, he said he was in a rush but still helped me to look for the right platform. The second experience was that, as it was winter, a cold wind was blowing. I was not used to such a cold climate and I was not prepared for it. I was wearing a suit without a jumper or a coat. My teeth were chattering and my hands were frozen. I couldn't put my hands in the pockets because I was holding my suitcase. I remember hiding behind posts and people in order to get some warmth. I was glad when the train for Southampton came. I got in and sat and enjoyed the warmth.

The train left at 12. I was told to look out for Southampton after the train had left Winchester. When the train went past Winchester I started looking out for Southampton. After 15 minutes, I saw the sign for

Southampton but the train didn't stop. I became panicky. I didn't know what to do. I was wondering how I would get back to Southampton as that was where my ticket was for. I started sweating and went to the next carriage to ask as there was no one where I was sitting. Then I was relieved to be told that the last stop was 'Southampton Parkways' and that the train was stopping at 'Southampton Central'.

The train reached Southampton at one o'clock. I came out of the station and I thought someone from the hospital would come to fetch me. There was no one there. I waited for 30 minutes. No one had told me to phone the hospital when I reached the station. I decided to take a taxi to the hospital. Finally, I was at the hospital – a very long journey. The taxi driver dropped me in front of this large building and helped me get my luggage into the reception. I paid the driver and he left.

I introduced myself to the receptionist, who telephoned the matron. I was asked to go to see this medium-built lady dressed in a navy blue uniform in her office. When I went in and introduced myself, in return I got a shock. She said that she had already sent a letter of refusal, which had either reached me after I had already left Mauritius, or Mr Moosad had got it and didn't give it to me.

Then she said, 'You can stay here for the night and I'll give you a room. Because you are already here, I'll give you two options.' Probably she knew that foreign students had difficulty in understanding English at first. She was speaking to me nicely and clearly.

'The choice is yours. The first is that there is another hospital only few miles from here that does the same sort of nurse training. They are starting their next training in April, that is, in two weeks, and still have vacancies. You can go there and start your training. The second is that you can work with us as a nursing assistant until September and then start your training. What do you think?'

'As I'm already here, miss, I think I'll stay here.'

I didn't know how to address her until she told me to call her Matron.

'I've had a lot of Mauritians here and I must say that their records are very good. Seeing you, I think you can make a good team member.'

'Thank you, Matron. I'll try my best,' I replied.

'You will meet a few of them in the nurses' home or in the canteen. Talking of which, you must be hungry. I'll ask one of the nurses to take you to your room and then to the canteen.

She pressed a button on the table and talked into it. I found out later that it was an intercommunication system. 'Jane,' she said, 'can you ask Nurse Greer to come to see me please.'

After five minutes, a slim, tall English man knocked and came in.

'Conal, can you tell Mr Smith to get me a room key for the nurses' home. Then take Mr Rey to his room and then to the canteen.'

'Yes, Matron.'

When Mr Greer went to get a key, the matron said that the food in the canteen was free and there was talk of introducing a 'pay-as-you-eat' (PAYE) system. When that was introduced, the usual supply of sugar, milk, and bread in the nurses' home would be stopped.

'Take a few days' rest, look around a bit to familiarise yourself with the place and people, and I'll make arrangements for you to start on Monday. You must be short of money. I'll talk to Mr Smith and tell him to give you some money from petty cash and deduct it when you get you first pay at the end of the month. Satisfied?'

'Thank you very much, Matron. You're very kind,' I replied.

Mr Greer came in and I followed him to my room – 19 – with my suitcase. He gave me a key and told me to keep it safely. He then took me to the canteen and introduced me to a few members of staff. I was told that it was too late to have a main meal, but they were prepared to make me some sandwiches to take to my room. They mentioned that the time for tea was 5 till 6.30.

'Is it just a cup of tea you have?'

'No,' Mr Greer replied. 'You may know it as supper, but we call it teatime when you can have a piece of cake, biscuits, or sandwiches with a cup of tea.'

I've been eating sandwiches most of the time. When can I have a plate of curry and rice? I thought to myself.

'I'll take you to your room and you can have a good bath and a good night's sleep. I'll see you later.'

'Later? When later?'

'No, Prem. It is one way of saying 'bye.'

He left, but I was surprised that, being younger than me, he called me by my first name. Where was the respect for older people? I thought, only to be told later that everyone called each other by their first name in England.

I had a wash in the bathroom, had my sandwiches, lay down to relax and went into a deep sleep. I must have slept through the night. I was awakened by the noise of the cleaner hoovering. I was still in my clothes and the suitcase was still standing by the table where I left it. I looked at my watch and it was nine o'clock – I had changed the time as soon as I set foot in England because Mauritian time was four hours ahead of English

90

time. I familarised myself with my room. It had a wardrobe, one table, one chair, one armchair, a bedside locker and a single bed. In one corner, there was a basin with hot and cold water taps and two towels to use. Along the window there was a radiator which was keeping the room warm. I looked through the window at the back and saw that there was a large garden. People were working in it. I also saw some people with funny mannerisms walking about. Suddenly I thought of mental subnormality. I thought that those people with funny mannerisms might be some of those patients. I looked on the other side and found that most of the trees were standing bare as if they were dead.

I unpacked some of my clothes and hung them in the wardrobe and changed into different clothes. I was feeling hungry and, as I was waiting for 12 o'clock when it would be time for dinner, as I had been told, I looked at the letters and leaving presents given me by people at home. Devi and Anand had given me a nice pen and Seema had given me a nice photo frame with our photo in it. I must start writing to . . . I was saying to myself when there was a knock at the door. I opened it to see a man with a smile on his face who shook hands with me.

'Good morning. Are you Rey?'

One way of addressing one's peers or subordinates in Mauritius is calling them by their surnames without Mr or Miss as the prefix.

'Good morning, Mr. Yes I am. You must be Mauritian,' I said with a sigh of relief, thinking that I would now get to know things better.

'I'm Matt. Yes, I'm Mauritian. Can I come in?' He started talking to me in broken French.

'You are already in. Come and take a seat. Is Matt your first name or surname?' I asked.

91

'It's my first name. Everyone calls each other by their first name here. So you've to get used to it. What's your first name?'

'My name is Prem?'

'You've got to give yourself an English name because that way people will find it easy to address you. Call yourself Peter except for official purposes.'

I was surprised he gave me an assumed name. But I started using the name Peter from then on until I left the hospital five years later.

'Yes, Pauline told me about you and told me to help you with things around here.'

'Who's Pauline?' I asked.

'Oh! She's the matron. When she gets to know you, she'll tell you to call her by Pauline as well. Oh! That's a nice photograph you've got. Is she your wife?' Matt asked.

'No it's my fiancée, Seema. I'm hoping to go back, marry her, and bring her over here as soon I've settled in.'

'That'll be nice. I had a girlfriend in Mauritius and, when I came here, I met Mary and stopped writing to my girlfriend. Pauline is nice. She'll help you. Have you had any breakfast?' Matt asked.

'No, Matt. I was so tired that I got up too late for it.'

'You could have gone downstairs . . . I don't suppose you know it. Get ready. I'll show you around,' Matt said. 'Haven't you got a jumper or a coat? It's cold outside.'

'No, Matt,' I replied. 'I'll have to buy one later.'

'Come to my room,' he said. 'I'll give you a jacket and you can use it until you buy one for yourself. First, I'll take you to the kitchen downstairs where you can make yourself a drink or toast whenever you want to. They have stores of tea, coffee, milk and bread for the nurses living in.'

92

He continued talking until we met the lady who was hoovering the floors.

'Oh! This is Blondie. Blondie, this is Peter,' Matt said.

'Pleased to meet you,' Blondie replied. 'Blondie keeps this place clean and even cleans your room,' Matt continued, 'and empties the bins. We change bed sheets every week. Change your bed every Monday morning and leave the dirty sheets and towels outside. They will take them away for you and give you clean ones. Can't be bad, can it? Besides, you don't pay much for the room. It's all deducted from your pay. This is the lounge where you can watch television at your leisure.'

It was nice because it was the first time I would be able to watch television. He showed me how to change channels.

'Are there many Mauritians here?' I asked curiously.

'We've got four more. Some have completed their training and moved on. You'll meet them eventually. My room number is five. If I'm in, you can come to see me. I start at one today. After lunch, you can either go back to your room to have a rest or go and look around.'

I found out that Matt liked talking, probably because I was new, and he tried his best to help me. He gave me a jacket which looked funny on me.

'Don't worry about the look,' he said. 'Nobody will laugh at you.'

I made sure I had my room key with me before we went for a meal in the canteen. It was already 12.30 and I was looking forward to the food. We sat at a table which was occupied by two people already. He introduced me to them as Peter. We looked at the menu and, because I wasn't sure of the food, Matt ordered lamb chop with vegetables for me. They put the food in front of me and left. I waited and Matt said, 'You can start eating now.'

'I'm waiting for them to bring me rice or bread to eat with this,' I said.

'That's called English food. You don't get rice or bread. This is all you get,' he answered.

I picked up the knife and fork to eat, only to experience a disaster. I was trying to eat the peas with the fork and they kept on going from one side of the plate to another. In the end, Matt showed me how to scoop them with the fork. The worst part was when I tried to cut the lamb chop. It slipped and went on to somebody's plate.

'Hey! I don't want your lamb chop. I've got enough of my own,' he said.

'Probably the lamb is still alive,' another one said.

'Sorry,' I said.

Matt smiled and showed me how to cut the meat. I didn't have much problem after that. After the meal, we had pudding with custard and then coffee. Then Matt left for work.

The next two days I tried to go around the hospital and noticed that the nurses' home was attached to this big building which was called 'the mansion'. The nurses' home was on one side and the administrative area was on the other. The hospital grounds were large and contained 12 big buildings known as 'villas'. I also managed to go to the local village, found a post office and bought some air letters so that I could write back home to say that I had reached my destination.

I had not felt homesick because of the excitement of the new place, until I sat down to write about my experiences at the hospital and about Matt. Then I posted the letters.

I met Matt the next day. He introduced me to his girlfriend and to the rest of the Mauritians. One day he took me to the Department of Social Security to get my work permit as I was starting work as a nursing assistant. He also took me to a local bank and helped me to open an account. I had to give Mr Smith its number so that he could put my wages directly into my account – a different practice from Mauritius, where I got cash for my wages.

I had been walking in the hospital grounds and had again seen many people with odd mannerisms. I didn't take much notice of them. I hadn't thought that they would be walking about in the grounds because, as they were patients, they should be on the wards. I still didn't know anything about mental subnormality nor did Matt tell me anything about it, probably because either he didn't want to scare me off or he wanted me to find out about it in my own time.

I received a letter from the matron stating that I could start work on I Villa from Monday and that I should report to the charge nurse at ten in the morning. I was asked to go to the store and get myself a uniform consisting of two pairs of trousers, two shirts, a jacket, a jumper, an overcoat and six white coats. Matt helped me find these places and helped me choose a suitable size uniform.

'I Villa is a good ward. You'll like it. The charge nurse, Joe, is a nice guy and a friend of mine. He's Spanish and he likes Mauritians,' Matt reassured me.

Matt became one of my best friends, helping me whenever required. I missed him when he left the hospital for further training in another hospital after I had been there for three years, but he kept in touch.

10

---

*Work Experience in the Hospital and
Nurse Training*

On Monday, I got ready in my uniform. I couldn't have
my breakfast because my stomach was churning due to
fear of working in a hospital for the first time. I went to
I Villa at 9.30 with a white coat over my arm. It was cold
but I was sweating as I didn't know how it was going to
be, although Matt had reassured me that it was a nice
ward. I asked for the charge nurse. I was introduced to
a medium-built, bearded man.

'You must be Peter?' the charge nurse asked.

'Yes, sir.'

'I'm Joe. Pauline told me that you'll be working with
me. Matt told me about you.'

He took me into his office and asked one of the
nurses in a white coat to make a pot of tea for us. When
the nurse brought in the tea on a tray with some
biscuits, he introduced me to the nurse called Howard
and told me that I would be working with him. While
we were having our tea, he told me that the ward had
46 patients who had mental subnormality; it was a
branch of psychiatric nursing. He said that I didn't have
to know their names straightaway but I would know
them gradually.

'When they come to you, don't get scared. Although

96

they are big or grown up, they won't harm you. They are like children.'

After a long talk, he showed me around and told me to put my white coat on and stay and observe what they did. At first, I was scared when a huge six-footer approached and hugged me. The charge nurse told me to say 'hello' to him and he would be all right. I started liking the job and I was looking forward to going to work.

'When you do your training, you'll be working on almost all the wards in the hospital,' Joe said. 'That way, you'll get to know all aspects of mental subnormality.'

Two interesting things happened when I was on I ward. Every time I replied to Joe, I addressed him as 'sir' as a habit and a sign of respect. One day, he said, 'Peter, please don't call me "sir". I'm not knighted by the Queen, you know. My name is Joe. Call me Joe. We call everyone by their first name here.'

'Sorry. It's a habit.'

'I know. Don't worry about it. Just call me Joe.'

The next thing was when Joe asked me to make tea. I went into the kitchen and was there for ten minutes. He came to see why I was taking such a long time. I was making tea the Mauritian way. I boiled the water in the kettle, opened it and put tea leaves and milk in it. I was about to add sugar when he walked in.

'What are you doing?' he asked.

'I'm making tea.'

'That's not the way we make tea.' I was sad to see that he threw everything away and showed me the right way of making tea – the English way.

It was September when I was asked to take a test in the School of Nursing based in the mansion. I was glad that I passed and was allowed to take the three-year course which, with success and experience, would lead to promotion and a chance for further training in other areas of nursing. Mr Clarke, the tutor, took the class, with ten students, including myself. I was glad that Conal and Howard were also in the group. We did the induction course for the first two weeks, which entailed introduction to mental subnormality and lectures by doctors and different charge nurses. I was sent to different wards and also on night duty. I didn't like night duty because, instead of enjoying day activities, I used to spend the time in bed.

It was difficult to understand people speaking to me. This was made worse when people came from different parts of the country. I remember that once I had to face people from the north of England, Devon and Ireland on one ward, with all their accents. It was most difficult to understand the person from Ireland. The only thing I could understand were rude words, which Mary used very often. They told me to watch more television and read a lot of books in order to be able to understand the accents. It took me at least six months to understand some of them.

I was becoming homesick more often because I was missing everyone at home, especially Seema. One day I went off sick and told the tutor that I was homesick.

He called me to the office and said, 'Mr Rey, we didn't ask you to come here, did we?'

'No, Mr Clarke.'

'You came here of your own accord and you've to get used to it. I'm sure all the Mauritians before you felt the same way. If you go off sick, you'll feel worse. It's best you come to the classes because this is your future. You miss a lot by not coming in unless you are genuinely sick, in which case we'll help you catch up with your studies.'

I was grateful that he talked to me like that.

Before I entered my second year training, I was approached by the male evening receptionist at the hospital. He said that he had noticed that I was free most evenings and asked me if I would like to work in a local Working Men's Club some evenings. He said that work would earn me 'some pennies' and that I would get free drinks. I thought that I would give it a try, not because I would have free alcoholic drink but because I could meet and socialise with people.

I worked there for a few weeks. I had to serve drinks from the dispensers and when I was serving, people used to tell me to serve one drink for myself. I had to take orders from people at the tables. Later on, I had to pick up dirty glasses and wash them as there was no dishwashers at that time. I worked for three hours per night and I never had the time to relax. All this was for £2 for the night in the early seventies. In the end, I had to give it up because the place was too crowded and full of smoke, which I could not bear, and also because of the hard work.

When I was still working there, I met a charge nurse from another villa. George and his friends used to go there most evenings. When I went to work on George's ward, after I had left my part-time job, he asked me if I would like to join them for a drink at another local pub. Because I had to work with him and I didn't want to be in his bad books, I agreed to join the group. The procedure was that each person would buy a round of drinks. I got hooked on alcoholic drinks, starting from the time I was working at the club, and it became a lunch-time and evening event. Most of the time I was going without food and got drunk. Then I remembered that Uncle Cheung had advised me not to mix with the wrong crowd. But it was difficult to judge whether a crowd was right or wrong until one mixed with it. The money in my bank account was getting low and I decided to find excuses for not going to the pubs.

When I entered the second year of my training, I wanted to take my six weeks' holiday, go to Mauritius, marry Seema and bring her to England. After I came to England, Seema had started taking tuition for GCE 'O' levels and managed to get five subjects, including English language. I talked to the matron and she told me to take my holiday, go home, get married and bring Seema to England. She also told me to ask Seema to write to her so that she could write back accepting her for training at the hospital as they were always short of staff. She emphasised that there was no married accommodation in the hospital, but I could use a double room that was available. I accepted the offer and told Seema to write to the matron, which she did, and the matron sent her a letter of acceptance. I was so elated that I thought that, at last, I was beginning to see the light at the end of the tunnel as my father had said.

Devi was pleased, and she mentioned in her letter that uncle was pleased, as well as Mr and Mrs Cheung. Jack used to write to me but this became irregular after he started a teaching job in Curepipe, a town a few miles from where he lived. My colleagues were also pleased that I was going to see them and get married there. I had sent some money to uncle and to Devi as a contribution towards my marriage. They said that I shouldn't have bothered because it was their duty to pay for my wedding. Besides, Seema's dad, as well as Uncle Cheung, wanted to help uncle. As uncle was living in Belle-Vue-Maurel, I had to go there instead of Madame Louis, our old place.

11

Start of a New Life

It was the beginning of my third year of training when I took six weeks (one week was a complimentary holiday from the matron) at the beginning of November. I went back to Mauritius by Sabena, the Belgian airline.

Mauritius airport was not modernised as it is now. The plane used to land and stop few hundred yards from the terminal building, and passengers would get off and walk to the building. It was fun to look out for relatives in the crowd who used to go on the viewing place on top of the building to wave at the arriving or departing passengers. Also, lots of people used to go to collect their relatives in hired cars or buses. Once the airport was modernised, all this changed.

It was ten in the morning and the plane stopped where it was expected and all the passengers walked to the customs and the arrival lounge. On the way, everyone was waving. Some had spotted their relatives and others had not, yet were still waving. I managed to spot Devi and Seema. Devi was wearing a red dress and Seema yellow. We went through the passport office and the customs and I was out within 40 minutes. I was overjoyed to see uncle, the Cheungs and some of my ex-colleagues who came to welcome me at the airport. We started talking as if there was no end to it.

101

'You have put on some weight,' was the first comment from Devi.

'Save some talk for later,' uncle said. 'Let's go home so that Prem can have a rest.'

The journey from the airport was different because the roads in Mauritius weren't as smooth and straight as in England. It was also different because, when I was leaving for England by ship, I had to travel to Port-Louis, which was only 15 miles from home. The airport was over 30 miles away in the south of Mauritius, a few miles from where I first worked. We came home along the east coast and it took us over an hour.

Once at home, I could not rest because there were many people there, including some of uncle's neighbours. I was surprised to see that uncle had added two more rooms to the original two-bedroomed house. It was nice because he could accommodate more people there. Everyone, except for Devi and Anand, left by four o'clock. Seema also left because it was not the custom for unmarried people to live together, although I met her quite often at her parents' place, but, because she was going to England, I saw her in the city as well.

When everybody left, Devi hugged me and said, 'Prem you're going to be an uncle soon.'

'Oh yea,' was my reply, a usual reply from England. 'That's nice. I'm thrilled.'

'Don't worry, we'll send you a photo of the baby.'

'I hope that you'll look after it well. I also hope that you'll tell him or her all about us,' I said.

'I will, Prem. That will be my priority,' Devi reassured me.

I spent the first week visiting my friends and relatives. Jack was engaged to a teacher where he worked and was hoping to get married soon. I also went to see my old place of work. The road was completed and in use

102

and they had named one of side roads Prem Avenue. All the workers had moved to a site in Triolet, in the north-east of the island and nearer home for all the workers.

At the end of the first week, uncle came to talk to me just like he used to do before I went away.

'Prem, you know that you don't have a long holiday. As you have come to get married, I think it's best to invite Seema's parents and others to arrange a date for the wedding.'

'I had left it with you, uncle,' I said with the same respect as before.

'I think we'll hold a meeting on Sunday. Is that all right?'

'Yes, uncle. Then I'll have the chance to invite my friends as well,' I said.

'It's all right then. Let me tell you something, Prem. You haven't changed a bit. You're the same Prem I knew two or nearly three years ago. I hope you'll never change.'

'How can I change, uncle? I know my past life. I've lived a simple life and I'll stay simple. I know some people get involved with the wrong crowd and live different lives, as Mr Cheung told me.' I was careful not to mention my temporary drinking problem with George and company.

'You're good, son.'

'Thank you, uncle.'

He said that he noticed that I was saying 'please' and 'thank you' more often. I told him that it was English etiquette.

Uncle held a family meeting on the second Sunday. Devi came on the eve to help prepare the meal for the guests. During the meeting, the date for the wedding was fixed for the thirtieth of November – three days before I was due to return to England. This gave me the chance to invite my friends and also the chance to complete the necessary arrangements for Seema to go to England with me. She was lucky to get a seat on the same flight.

The wedding preparations were in full swing. Uncle had joined a local club (the Nehru Bhawan Society) and the members helped pitch a tent in front of the house and cook meals for the guests. This was the first time I had experienced the real wedding procedure – Mauritian style. I considered my wedding to be a real Mauritian one because, although I had assisted other weddings, such as those of my cousins Koosh and Parm and of Anand and Devi, they were not the same. The weddings of Koosh and Parm were not the same because, firstly, uncle, being on his own, was just about able to afford the two weddings and, secondly, we lived in a remote place and uncle did not invite many people. I didn't know much of Anand and Devi's because I went there on Sunday in time for the ceremony and because uncle couldn't go there on Saturday. Besides, Devi was too excited to have met her long lost brother to tell me about the eve.

Weddings were usually held on a Sunday because that was the only day people had the chance to attend them. Generally bands were hired and music blared from loudspeakers placed outside so that the whole village could hear it. There was no concern about annoying the neighbours because everyone got invited. On the eve of the wedding, a dinner party was held, after which musicians played and then the women got together and sang and danced.

On the day of the wedding, many friends arrived and, after having a meal, I dressed in the same clothes Anand had got married in. I was surprised that the

104

trousers fitted me. I got into a specially decorated car, and uncle and Anand came with me. Uncle was to stand as my father and Anand as the best man. Devi had to stay behind because, as was the custom, women couldn't travel in the procession. I would have asked her to come with us but she was involved entertaining relatives who were left behind. Ten cars, including mine, left for the same village hall where Devi had got married. Uncle Cheung used his own car. He took his wife with him because he didn't want to come back.

We left Belle-Vue-Maurel at ten o'clock. We didn't go through the way we used to go to work, but through Port-Louis and reached Rose Belle at 11.30. After the initial reception, the wedding started at 12.

The hall was decorated and on the wall where we were getting married there was a fancy sign: 'CON-GRATULATIONS TO PREM AND SEEMA'. Seema looked stunning in a red sari and I supposed I looked all right in my clothes.

The wedding started with the priest welcoming the guests. He congratulated me for coming back from England to get married to a Mauritian girl amidst my friends and relatives. The ceremony lasted for 45 minutes. I was supposed to sit there crossed-legged but I couldn't do it due to loss of practice. They gave us cane chairs to sit on. I supposed this was better than sitting with legs crossed for over 30 minutes. A photographer, who was hired for the occasion, was busy taking our photos for everything different we did during the ceremony.

After the wedding, Anand volunteered to give a speech. I thought he was going to give me some sort of surprise as I did during his wedding. Instead, he congratulated us for the wedding and also said how pleased everyone was to see me getting married after being in

105

England for a couple of years. At the end, he announced that Seema and I were leaving on Wednesday and would meet the relatives again then, as we might not have the chance to make another trip to see them.

Then everybody was asked to proceed to Seema's place, where a meal would be served. Everyone followed our car. When we arrived, everyone came to see us. Seema and I wanted to change to our casual clothes, but we had to wait until we went back to Belle-Vue-Maurel. Bobby, Devi's adopted brother, was there talking to me about his girlfriend. Seema and I went to meet the Cheungs as they were leaving. I promised to go and see them the following day. Some of my guests had also left. In the end, we took leave of Seema's parents, went to Devi's place for a quick visit and left for home, uncle with Seema and me at the back and Anand in the front. It was also the custom to have a woman relative to accompany the bride after the wedding. In our case, Seema's grandmother came. We were home by five.

When we reached home, there was a group waiting for us, with Devi in the front with two flower garlands to welcome Seema and me. After the reception, we were glad to change into our casual clothes. A small party was held, after which everyone drifted away and we all went to bed tired.

The next day uncle, Anand and Devi, Seema and her escort, and I went to Seema's place. We had a meal and left, leaving Seema behind to spend the last two days with her parents before going to England with me. We went to see the Cheungs and then left for home, telling them that we would be leaving on Wednesday at two to be in time for the check-in and that the plane was leaving at five o'clock. They said that they would come along with Devi's as well as Seema's parents to meet us at the airport.

We all went to Port-Louis on Tuesday to do some shopping. No one bought me any presents because I had enough from the wedding. I didn't buy anything for anyone but preferred to give them some money. We were back home by five and, at six, a lorry stopped, and there were all the friends. They said that they wanted to see me then although they were tired.

Alan, the driver, said, 'We're glad that you haven't forgotten us. Now you're married, we hope that you'll still remember us.'

The meeting was emotional and I said, 'Friends, I'll never forget any one of you. No matter what happens, I'll always keep in touch with you. By the way, how is Mr Tate?'

'Well. He's left the company now. I saw him in town one day and he asked me about you,' said Toon.

'I didn't manage to get his address before I left. Please give him my regards when you see him next time.'

'We will do.'

On Wednesday morning, I got up early and, before breakfast, I went to Madame Louis, my old place. Uncle had left my old house standing. I went in and spent 30 minutes there thinking about the old days. When I was coming out, I was surprised to see Devi and Anand coming in. They must have followed me. We hugged and Devi said, 'I hope this place will stay up as long as nature lets it.'

'I hope so as well,' I replied.

'This will remind us of the old days,' Devi added.

'I know,' I said.

107

'We are thinking of erecting a memorial here with our parents' names engraved on it. It will be a marble one and Anand has agreed to help.'

'That will be nice. I'll help as well,' I said.

We left and went through Barlow to meet the shop-keeper where uncle still bought his 'ration'. We came home, had our breakfast, and started getting ready to leave home at one. We used Anand's car and were at the airport at 2.15. Everyone else was there already. I had told Seema that, as it was winter in England, she should carry a coat with her and not to wear it because, as it was summer in Mauritius, it was hot.

We checked in. Seema didn't have any problem with the visa because she had her letter from the matron. We went through, then outside to the plane. We waved back and got in the plane. Seema couldn't stop crying because she was leaving her loved ones behind. I was emotional but not as much as the first time.

We arrived at the hospital and went to the double room the first day. It was strange living with a female companion but I soon got used to it.

Matt came to see me the same evening. I took Seema to see the matron the next day. She was pleased to see her and wished her luck in her new life. When we were talking, she gave me some shocking news.

'Prem,' she said, 'I'm leaving for Scotland in two weeks.'

'Why is it, Matron,' I asked. I still didn't call her Pauline because she hadn't told me to do so.

'Well, I've been here a long time. I got a job there and I think I'll move on.'

'We'll miss you, Matron,' I said sadly. 'If I don't have the chance to meet you before that, I wish you good luck.'

'I wish you and your pretty wife good luck as well.'

'Thank you, Matron, for everything you've done for me,' I said.

'You're welcome. Mr Rogers is replacing me. I hope you'll get on all right with him. See you later.'

I thought it was too much of a coincidence when Matt told that he was leaving as well. He was going to do general nursing in Surrey. I told him how I had appreciated his help, especially when I was new at the hospital, and that I would miss his company. He left, but we never stopped contacting each other by letter or by phone.

Seema had an interview with Mr Clarke and she was due to start her training in January. It was not worth starting work as a nursing assistant because of the hassle of having a work permit, so she was advised to enjoy herself till then.

In January, when Seema was due to start her training, the law changed and the name of mental subnormality was changed to mental handicap. Also, as part of her training, Seema was required to work in an adult training centre in the community for a month. In addition to that, the provision of bread, milk, tea, coffee and bread in the nurses' home was stopped as the system of pay-as-you-eat was introduced. This meant that we had to pay when we had our meals in the canteen (the name was changed to restaurant) instead of having it deducted from our pay whether we ate or not.

Seema and I got on well. We couldn't go anywhere during her first year in England because I was taking my examinations and she was getting to know the place. I passed my examinations, and the hospital appointed me as a qualified nurse deputising as a charge nurse on L Villa – a ward for adolescents.

12

New Pangs of Life

I was in my third year as a deputy when there was a chance for promotion to charge nurse. Seema had just started her third year training. She was doing community work as part of her training, at an adult training centre for the patients at nine in the morning. She had to leave home at 7.30 and finished at five in the afternoon. The hospital didn't provide transport, so she used to catch a bus and get home by 6.30 in the evening. She came home on time the first week. I used to cook food – we had the chance to cook in the nurses' home kitchen – and wait for her at the bus stop and we walked home together.

During the second week, I waited for her at the stop as usual. The bus came and went and there was no sign of Seema. The next bus came and went and there was still no sign of her. I waited for the third bus – buses ran half-hourly – and she was on it. When I asked her what had happened, she said that she went to a party. I didn't take much notice of it because she could have gone with her work colleagues. I told her that she could have telephoned me at the nurses' home or on my ward to say that she would be late. She said that she didn't think of it then. She didn't eat that evening. After that day, she was late coming home for a few evenings. Her excuses

110

were that they were either working late or were holding meetings.

Seema's attitude towards me was not the same after she went on the community placement. She was snappy and wouldn't discuss things with me. At first I thought it was her examinations, but she took them and was successful yet she didn't change. By this time, I was working as a charge nurse and had got a permanent visa. Because of me, she also got a permanent visa.

One evening, when I came home from work, Seema wasn't there. I thought she had gone shopping or somewhere with some friends. She hadn't cooked nor left any message for me. This reminded me of the time I was separated from Devi when she was adopted. I didn't want to panic as she might turn up and it would have been a case of much ado about nothing. It was getting late and I decided to go to bed, hoping that she would turn up. At home I had uncle to talk to, but here I couldn't see anyone to ask for advice. Matt had gone and there was no one else I could think of. I couldn't sleep because I was thinking what could have happened to Seema.

The next morning I went to work although I was feeling tired. I had wanted to take sick leave, but I still didn't want to over-react. When I went to work, the nursing officer telephoned me to go to M Villa because Mr Young had not come to work. I went there and, when I was talking to the staff, I was told that Mr Alan Young had not even telephoned to say that he was off sick. An odd notion came to my mind that led me to think, Could there be any connection between Alan and Seema? With this thought, I decided to let nature take its course. In those days we had telephones in post offices and police stations in Mauritius and, if there was an emergency, we could ask the respective officers to

111

tell our people to await our calls at a certain time. I didn't want uncle, Devi, or Seema's parents to get worried. I continued writing letters as if nothing had happened.

After the second day, I started getting panicky. I talked to someone and I was told to contact the Salvation Army for missing people and they would help me find Seema. I found an address and wrote to them. They sent me a form to fill in and return with a fee. They advised me not to do anything until I heard from them. After a week they told me that they had located Seema and that reconciliation wasn't possible.

All sorts of ideas started coming to my mind. I wondered what could have gone wrong. If she had problems, she could have talked to me about them. I also wondered if she could have gone away with Alan Young. He had still not come back to work so I could not talk to him. Now I remembered the times when she came back late from her community work. Their relationship might have started then. Instead of telling me the truth, she was giving me excuses.

One day I decided to telephone Devi in Mauritius and find out if Seema had contacted them. I preferred to telephone the police station, which, she had told me, was more private than the post office. She said to me that her son, Sanjay, now three, had started talking. Uncle had not been too well, Anand had a teaching job in Belle-Vue-Maurel, and they had moved into the house with uncle so that they could look after him.

'How are you keeping? Where's my friend Seema,' Devi asked.

'We're fine, Devi,' I answered. 'Seema is working. I've got three weeks' holiday and I'd like to come to see you all. Seema couldn't get a holiday but she doesn't mind me going on my own. Is it okay?' I asked.

'It's okay. I'll talk to you then, 'bye,' Devi replied.

I managed to book my holiday. I bought some presents for my friends and relatives, and went to Mauritius three weeks after I had talked to Devi on the phone. I met Sanjay. He looked cute and chatty. Uncle was ageing and couldn't walk properly and Devi had hired people to work on our farm. One day I went for a walk to Madame Louis and Devi followed me.

'Prem. What's wrong?' she asked. 'I can see something is bothering you.'

'Nothing, Devi,' I said.

'No, I can feel it. You can't lie to me.'

'I know. Why does it always happen to me.'

'What's happening, Prem?' Devi asked me coolly.

I told her what had happened and that, because we didn't have any children, we could be divorced soon.

'I can't believe my best friend has done that to me. She knows our story, and you have been so nice to her,' Devi said angrily and added, 'What are you going to tell her parents?'

'I think I'm going to tell them the same thing I told you, that she couldn't have a holiday, and let her contact them. I thought she would have done so already.'

'I suppose that'll be all right. I don't think she has contacted them. They would have told me,' Devi reassured me.

'We won't say anything to anyone. We'll carry on as if nothing has happened,' I said.

'I'll have to tell Anand because I know he won't tell anyone,' Devi replied. 'Let's go back.'

We came back through Barlow and went to visit the shop where uncle still bought his 'ration'. The shopkeeper I knew before had died and his son had taken over the business. We came home and saw uncle feeding Sanjay and Anand getting ready to go to work. Then we had our breakfast and started making plans to visit friends and relatives. Devi went to her room and told Anand the problem because, when he came out, he said he was sorry and he would talk to me later.

I went to see the Cheungs, Devi's parents, and Seema's parents. I had a snack at Seema's parents, and told them that Seema was all right and that she couldn't get her holiday, adding that I had to come because my holiday was overdue and I wanted to see everyone. The rest of my holiday was spent visiting my friends, seeing places I had never been to, buying and sending cards to friends in England, and buying souvenirs for friends.

While I was still there, Anand had a telephone installed because, he said, 'It will be nice that we can talk to you. Uncle isn't always well and a phone will help to contact the hospital if something happens to him. We have an ambulance service now, so we can call for an ambulance by phone.'

I visited my relatives a few more times, but my torment about Seema was affecting me a lot, although I was careful not to show my emotion to other people. The thought of the light at the end of the tunnel came to me. I began wondering whether the light I saw when I got married was an illusion or just never happened. The darkness had come back.

Three weeks went by and I came back to England. I told Devi that I was going to do further training. Six months after I came back from Mauritius, I applied to a hospital and moved to London to do general nurse training. There was still no sign of Seema nor did I know of her whereabouts. I decided to move on. After I completed my next training, I moved back to mental handicap nursing (now known as people with learning disabilities).

It was then I heard that Seema had contacted Devi from a temporary address in the west and wanted to have my address. Seema said to Devi that she was sorry that she had acted stupidly and that she wanted to come back to me – after an absence of five years. Devi phoned me to give me the news and advised me to be careful. Seema had also contacted her parents, saying that she had made a mistake and that she wanted to patch things up with me. At this time, I had already got a divorce because I had the proof from the Salvation Army that she didn't want to come back. I told Devi to give Seema my address but I said that I wouldn't get back together with her.

Once she received my address, Seema came to see me unexpectedly. She had two children – a three-year-old boy and a two-year-old girl. Although I had wanted her back, this changed my mind. I talked to her and she said that Alan had gone off with someone else and that she hadn't seen him for a long time. She talked to me, hoping that I would take her back. I said that I would think about it and, if she gave me her address, I would contact her. She said that she would get in touch with me, and that was the last time I heard from her or saw her.

I went back for another holiday in Mauritius. This time I was glad that everyone knew about my marriage. Seema's parents apologised to me on her behalf. They urged me to get married to another girl, but I preferred to give it a miss for the time being for fear that history might repeat itself.

'I've gone through a lot,' I said to Devi. 'I can't take any more.'

There were a lot of changes in Mauritius. The airport was improved and, instead of coming out of the plane and walking a few yards in the open before entering customs, the plane came to the side of the building and passengers went straight to customs, just like in England. It was nice when people were able to wave at relatives before and, because everything had changed, people thought it a waste of time going in groups to drop or pick up passengers, although some people maintained the custom. Buses and cars had increased on the roads. Computers had been introduced and they were making a big impact. Tourism was becoming a successful industry. There were a lot of jobs around. These changes made me think of going back to Mauritius for good.

13

Change of Lifestyle

I applied for a nursing job in Mauritius and got it. I passed the medical test and was given two months to start work in the Mauritian psychiatric hospital. Then I thought that, if the computer industry was looking for people to work there, I would rather go to work as a computer operator than to go there as a nurse. So I changed my mind and decided to do a part-time computer programming course in London. I left the nursing profession and went to work in a well-known travel agency whilst doing the course at weekends. I also had to find accommodation after living in nurses' homes for all my life in England. It was not easy because, when living outside, I had to pay for all my bills, whereas I only had to pay for the room in the nurses' home.

I started to like the job at the travel agency. It was a Monday-to-Friday job, which suited me well for the computer course. Problems arose when the travel agency eventually closed down and everyone was surprised at the sudden decision.

I became unemployed because I was not offered an alternative job nor was I given any redundancy pay as I had not been there long enough. I was receiving unemployment benefit and had to discontinue my computer course. Later, I got a job in another office and, after three months, the company moved to a different area and I couldn't move with them. Then I moved to a third office which was also moving.

I had always kept in touch with Matt. At this time he was a nursing officer in a hospital for people with learning disabilities. Because I was having problems with employment, he urged me to join the hospital where he was working. He said that they were short of staff on night duty and that the night staff were well paid. I was convinced and joined the hospital, and lived in the nurses' home. Matt was married and living in a three-bedroom house with his Mauritian wife and three children. After working for two years on night duty at the hospital, I bought a three-bedroom house and moved in there.

When I left the nursing profession to work in the travel agency, I also started studying for GCE 'A' level. I continued with my studies when I moved to the hospital where Matt was working, and there didn't seem to be an end to it. When I joined the hospital, Matt continued calling me Peter. I told him that I was known as Prem by then, but he didn't seem to stop.

When I got to the hospital, I met a Mauritian lady called Rosa. She helped me a lot and even stopped people calling me Peter. I learned to live a better life through her. We were so close that people thought that we were husband and wife. People suggested that we got married, but the thought of Seema spoilt everything.

I had been working on night duty at the hospital for 15 years when it was announced that the hospital was closing down. It was a real blow to me when I thought I was settling down. However, I was given the option of either going on day duty or taking redundancy money and leaving. As I had worked on night duty for many years because of my studies and had got used to it, I preferred to leave.

I became unemployed and looked for another job working on night duty. I joined a nursing agency, a company run by an ex-colleague. I worked in a nursing home for a while until I got a security officer's job on night duty. This job seemed to fit in with my studies and my lifestyle.

Something else had been upsetting me a lot for the last few years. I was addicted to playing fruit machines. It became such an addiction that I was playing hundreds of pounds at any one time. This reminded me of the time I was addicted to alcohol when I was mixing with George and his friends. It wasn't mixing with the wrong crowd this time. I decided it was either greed at the prospect of winning a jackpot or the thought of Seema, which struck me as depression, that made me resort to the machines and got me addicted to them.

I played the machines for some years and couldn't save much money. It was affecting my studies and I wasn't doing well with my assignments. One day, after having a bad time with the machines, I came out of the arcade and promised myself that I wouldn't go back to it. I wrote the date on a piece of paper and put it on my notice board. I had made such promises before but the note on my board did the trick.

CONCLUSION

Devi had urged me to go back to Mauritius, but I kept on telling her that I had been in England for more years than I had been in Mauritius. I knew that some of my friends had gone back but returned because they could not adapt to the different style of life in Mauritius. I was used to the way of life in England and thought I wouldn't be happy in Mauritius. I also told her that I knew she was there and that I'd contact her whenever I needed to. She had two children – Sanjay, who was 12, and Helen, who was 8.

Uncle passed away after suffering from his old disease, diabetes. I went to Mauritius after his death. My cousins Koosh and Parm were now grandparents. Koosh had three daughters and one son, all married, and Parm had four daughters and four sons, and they were all married as well. Devi's adopted parents were still alive but they were getting on a bit and so were Anand's parents. Bobby, Devi's adopted brother, got married and also had two children. Mr and Mrs Cheung were still there, but didn't go to work. Jack, who was married with a son, had left his teaching job and was working full-time in the shop. Some of my friends had stopped writing to me, but I still tried to visit as many as I could when I visited Mauritius. Our farm was intact and we were still hoping to build a memorial with our parents' names engraved on it. Every time I went to Mauritius, I never failed to visit the village hall at Rose Belle because this was where I found my long-lost sister Devi and my ex-wife Seema.

This is the story of my life, which is full of miseries. I have the determination to live through depression although urges to end my life have occurred. I owe allegiance to two people. Firstly, I am grateful to my uncle, who was determined to give my sister and me the best we could have in our lives. Secondly, I am thankful to my sister, who helped towards such a magnificent career and advised me especially when Seema left me. Her love for me has become an unending edifice of life. I might find another person to love but I have adopted a certain lifestyle and a break from it might bring further problems in my life. Some friends said that I might not know the difference unless I tried it. But I had tried and I suffered for it. It is said that it docs not rain but it pours. It has certainly never stopped pouring in my case. I want to stop recurrences of further separation but, at the same time, I would require a life partner whom I can trust and enjoy the the rest of my life with. I'm still working as a security officer and, at the same time, continuing with further studies. Some people have asked me how I do it. I always say that I'm used to it and where there is a will there is a way. I'll continue in this spirit, hoping that the light at the end of the tunnel will appear for real and stay forever. But the question remains: when will it appear?